THE
ABERDARE
RAILWAY

by
Eric R. Mountford
and
R.W. Kidner

THE OAKWOOD PRESS

© Oakwood Press

British Library Cataloguing in Publication Data
A Record for this book is available from the British Library
ISBN 0 85361 474 1

Typeset by Oakwood Graphics.

Printed by Henry Ling Ltd, The Dorset Press, Dorchester

The unusually wide island platform at Abercynon; the engine shed can just be seen at far
right.   *Berry, Aberdare*

Published by
The Oakwood Press
P.O. Box 122, Headington, Oxford OX3 8LU

Author's Note

Unlike most other valleys in east South Wales which conveniently run north to south, the Aberdare or Cynon Valley runs from south-east to north-west. For clarity, the railways through the valley have been describes as running west or east.

Another problem arose over what name to call the main valley. Valleys are normally named after the river that runs through them, such as Rhondda, Rhymney etc. The Aberdare valley is, however, so widely known by that name that it is so called in this history, although the author is only too well aware that many local inhabitants prefer it to be known, correctly, as the Cynon Valley, hence apologies are due to local readers for the choice of name.

Finally, so many collieries, also a few railway locations, had a slight change of name over the years, usually from the Welsh spelling to its English form, that it was difficult to decide which spelling to use. As far as possible this has followed the spelling used on maps and official documents at the time in question. There is one major exception - Duffryn - which in the nineteenth century was usually spelled Dyffryn. As so many collieries incorporated this name, and as some maps of the late 19th century used both spellings, it was thought better if the latter spelling was used throughout.

The great export coal trade from South Wales brought the rise of Cardiff from a comparatively minor harbour to one of the world's leading docks, due in no small measure to the efforts of the miners in the Aberdare valley, and also to the Taff Vale Railway for transporting the coal to Cardiff for shipment. Of the 31 TVR mineral trains daily to Cardiff in 1860, no less than 20 were from the Aberdare valley. By 1854 over one million tons of coal annually was being raised in the valley, and this had risen to well over two million tons by 1862. The trade recessions over the next 12 years or so kept the annual totals to around this figure. But in the 1880s they began to climb again and over three million tons were raised in 1889 and five years later a total of over four million tons had been exceeded.

Following the initial success of the Aberdare coalfield practically every other valley in the area joined the great stampede to raise coal to the surface. The boom continued until World War I and during 1913 no less than 56,830,072 tons of coal were raised in South Wales, of which 38,851,255 were shipped by the South Wales ports.

By the early 1870s the neighbouring Rhondda valley had overtaken the Aberdare valley as the leading coalfield in South Wales, and in 1875 the valley suffered a further blow when, following a trade depression aggravated by a prolonged coal strike, the iron industry closed down in the area. The ironworks collieries continued in production, however, and brighter times for the coalfield were ahead; the Aberdare valley continued to be a major coal producing area until the severe trade recession of the late 1920s and early 1930s when many of the valleys' pit cages came up for the last time. As late as 1924 more than 21,000 colliers were employed in the valley and at various times during the first quarter of the present century as many as 13 collieries employed over 1,000 men each.

As in the rest of the South Wales coalfield, the industry declined in the Aberdare valley from the 1930s onwards. Apart from Penrhiwceiber, all the pits left working belonged to the enlarged Powell Duffryn Associated Collieries Ltd, which had taken over Nixons Navigation at Mountain Ash in 1936.

[The author originally concluded his introductory note with a description of the further run-down of the collieries; at the time this book is being prepared for press (1994), the one colliery surviving, Tower at Hirwaun, which had never been connected to the Aberdare Railway, was closed, but was re-opened in 1995.]

Publisher's Note

The late Eric Mountford compiled this history between 1971 and 1973, with the assistance of Neil Sprinks and other friends. His position as officer of the GWR and BR in the Cardiff area up to 1980 gave him access to many sources of information on history and working. The present book includes some additional notes from Colin Chapman and Roger Kidner, derived from the Minutes, press reports and maps in the National Library of Wales, and from John F. Mear of Gadlys, Aberdare.

A class '37' diesel engine setting back a train from Abercynon into the former Nixons complex, now sadly overgrown, in May 1971. The former TVR Oxford Road station is at the right; the derelict NCB steam engine shed is just above the front wagons.

Tom Heavyside

Contents

A view of Aberaman station, looking towards Aberdare, 25th August, 1959.
M. Hale/ C. Chapman Collection

Mountain Ash Bridge.

Cwmpennar & George Collieries.

The Cwm Pennar and George collieries were on the east side of the valley, but connected across the GWR to the TVR at Deep Duffryn. *Ian Pope Collection*

Chapter One

Iron and Coal Found in the Valley

At the commencement of the 19th century Aberdare was a peaceful and somewhat isolated village of a few hundred people lying near the head of the Aberdare valley (now more generally known as the Cynon valley), near the point where the tributary River Dare joins the River Cynon. The valley, a little under eight miles in length, connected at the south-eastern end with the Taff valley at Navigation House (now Abercynon) and throughout its length was covered with fine oaks which majestically overlooked the river that wound its way down the valley to join the River Taff, also near Navigation. The whole of the Taff valley was also well populated with fine oak and elm trees, and it was said to be possible for a squirrel to travel from Penderyn, some five miles north-west of Aberdare, right through the Aberdare and Taff valleys as far as Llandaff, on the outskirts of Cardiff, without the need to touch the ground.

Minor attempts to disturb the solitude of the valley had been made much earlier. A small charcoal furnace (remains are extant) had been set up near Cwmaman, in the short tributary Aman valley, in the 16th century, and one was certainly started at Llwydcoed, about 1½ miles north-west of Aberdare village, in 1663. Little more is known of either, and it was not until 1750 that there were further signs of industrial life when, it was later reported, a 22 inch seam of coal was being worked in a small way at Craig y Duffryn, some 250 yards higher up the slope of the hillside than the later famous Middle Duffryn colliery. Shortly afterwards coal was also being worked at Cwm Pennar, near Mountain Ash, about half way down the valley, but these were all minor workings and the general atmosphere of the valley remained unchanged.

During 1757 a small charcoal furnace began operating at Hirwain, some 3½ miles north-west of Aberdare. Although this was developed into a major ironworks by Anthony Bacon in 1780, it had little effect on the Aberdare valley as its products were mainly taken over the mountain, by pack horse, to Merthyr Tydfil, and the tracks by-passed Aberdare. A proposal in 1798 to build a tramroad from Cardiff to the Carno Mill at Rhymney included a branch running westwards to Aberdare, but the project was abandoned; when a similar scheme was mooted 20 years later, resulting in the Rumney Tramroad, Aberdare was ignored, as it was also by the 1801 Penydarren Tramroad, on the east bank of the River Taff.

From 1800 onwards, however, life began to change in the Aberdare area. The previous year the brothers George and John Scale secured a lease on land at Llwydcoed, and and built the Aberdare Ironworks there which opened in 1801. A further ironworks was started by the partners Homfray and Birch at Abernant, on the north-eastern outskirts of Aberdare, about 1801. The following year Homfray and Birch took Messrs F. and R. Tappenden into partnership with them, and the transformation of the Aberdare area into the centre of a flourishing iron making area had begun in earnest. The Abernant

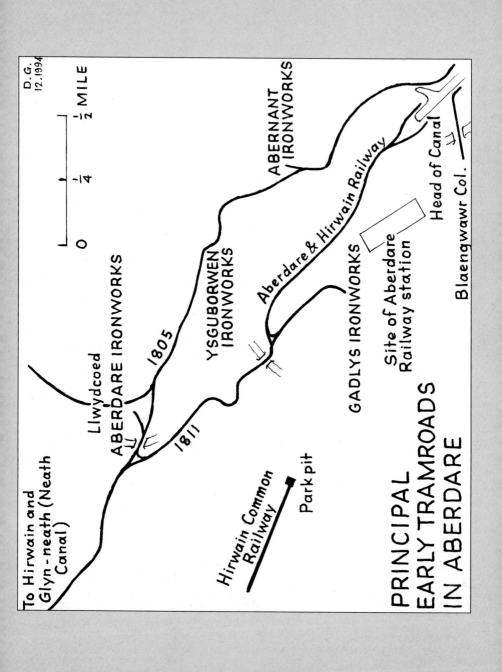

D.G.
12.1994

To Hirwain and
Glyn-neath (Neath
Canal)

Llwydcoed
ABERDARE IRONWORKS

1805

1811

YSGUBORWEN
IRONWORKS

ABERNANT
IRONWORKS

Aberdare & Hirwain Railway

GADLYS IRONWORKS

Hirwain Common
Railway

Park pit

Site of Aberdare
Railway station

Head of Canal

Blaengwawr Col.

0   ¼   ½ MILE

PRINCIPAL
EARLY TRAMROADS
IN ABERDARE

works were in full production by 1804, and had probably started producing in a small way the previous year. New villages sprang up around the ironworks and over the years these coupled with Aberdare village to form the nucleus of the later Aberdare UDC. Until 1805, however, the iron products had to be taken to Merthyr and Hirwain by pack horse, as no other form of transport was by then available in the locality.

Communications in the valley were virtually non-existent. Travellers from Cardiff could get as far as Navigation by gig, but could then only proceed into the valley by means of horse-drawn sledge cars, which had to traverse a most tortuous route up and down the mountain tracks to reach Aberdare. In the Taff valley the Glamorgan canal, which extended from Merthyr down the valley right through to Cardiff, had been opened throughout in 1794, whilst the Neath canal had been completed to Glyn Neath (then also called Abernant) the following year. In March 1793 the Aberdare Canal Act was passed authorising the construction of a canal from a junction with the Glamorgan canal, at Navigation, and thence through the Cynon valley to a point some ½ mile short of Aberdare village, together with a connecting tram road from that point (later to be known as Canal Head) to the Neath canal at Glyn Neath, the tram road to pass the ironworks at Hirwain.

With only one ironworks involved at the time, and none then contemplated in the Aberdare valley, nothing was done to construct the canal. It was not until 1805, following efforts made by the ironmasters at Llwydcoed and Abernant to obtain communication to their works, that a tramroad was constructed from the Neath canal, at Glyn Neath, to the Abernant works. This tramroad was routed via the Hirwain and Llwydcoed ironworks. It was financed by the proprietors at Abernant, with agreed tolls from the other two works, but was operated by the Neath Canal Company. Immediately west of Hirwain the tramroad connected with an earlier tramroad, originally put down in 1786, from the Hirwain works to Penderyn Quarry, and which had been moderrnised and extended southwards to some coal levels at Bryngwyn on Hirwain Common. Thus communication westwards from the three ironworks was established in 1805, although no such communication extended eastwards to the Taff valley and thence to the coast at Cardiff. Work had commenced on a turnpike road from Navigation to Glyn Neath, via Aberdare and Hirwain, in the spring of 1803, but the road was not finished until 1810.

Following further efforts to obtain communication with Cardiff the Aberdare Canal Company, in August 1809, agreed to construct the canal as authorised by the 1793 Act, together with a tramroad from Canal Head to the Llwydcoed works. Work commenced early in 1810 and the canal was opened for traffic in August 1812. The tramroad at Llwydcoed had been completed the previous year, passing the southern boundary of Aberdare village and joining the existing tramroad from Glyn Neath south of the Llwydcoed works.

In 1819 the Aberdare Iron Co. acquired the Abernant Works, and immediately constructed a direct tramroad from the Abernant Works to the Canal Head in order to avoid the long circular route, via Llwydcoed, which the Abernant traffic, destined for the Aberdare Canal, previously had to take. In

1823 Fothergill also acquired the Llwydcoed Works, afterwards trading as the Aberdare Iron Company.

A further small ironworks was started by G.R. Morgan, E.M. Williams and M. Wayne in Gadlys in 1827; it was later developed by the Waynes and had a branch line from the tramroad to the canal. The works was sited to the west of the existing Aberdare village, and only a short distance from the 1811 tramroad from Llwydcoed ironworks to Canal Head, hence it was a simple matter to lay down the short connection necessary to serve the new ironworks.

Thus by 1827 Aberdare had three ironworks in the immediate area, and all *could* send their products either westwards to the Neath canal, or eastwards to the Aberdare and Glamorgan canals. However, from the opening of the Aberdare canal practically all traffic from the Hirwain and Aberdare Works was routed eastwards and the tramroad west of Hirwain gradually fell into decay. Eventually, in 1841, the tramroad from Hirwain to Abernant was acquired by the Aberdare Canal Company.

Before that time, however, great excitement had been caused by the appearance of the first steam engine in the Aberdare area. This was one of several constructed as steam road vehicles by a Cornishman, Goldsworthy Gurney, who was persuaded by the Crawshay family, ironmasters at Merthyr and Hirwain, to bring one to South Wales. It was towed by horses from London to Cyfarthfa Castle, the home of the Crawshays, near Merthyr, towards the end of February 1830. It was fitted with cast-iron wheels and had a trial run on special track laid at the Castle, after which it was sent down to the Crawshays' Hirwain Common Railway (actually a plateway) at the head of the Cynon Valley, where the engine, which weighed only 35 cwt. hauled over 20 tons of iron at a speed of about 6 mph. This and possibly two other Gurney engines remained at work for a time, and were favoured by William Crawshay Junior, though not by his father.

Nevertheless the possibilities of steam haulage had been demonstrated, and Lord Bute's Agent wrote to the Crawshays concerning his hope of moving by steam large tonnages of coal from his pits at Aberdare to the Hirwain ironworks. From now on in parts of South Wales, steam locomotives began to shoulder burdens which had for 40 years been the lot of the horse. Steam locomotives had been seen at Tredegar, Dowlais and Merthyr before the Aberdare Railway's *Columbia* caused a great stir in the valley.

By the early 1840s 'sale coal' collieries, as distinct from coal raised for use in the ironworks, were springing up. Whilst near-surface coal had been worked in a small way in the valley for some years, the first deep mine was at Cwmbach, a mile or so down valley from Aberdare, which Thomas Wayne of the Gadlys works had started sinking in June 1837. The success of this pit, in particular the very fine quality of steam coal produced, led Thomas Powell to desert his haunts in Monmouthshire and start his Duffryn coal empire in the valley in February 1840. His first pit (Old Duffryn) was sunk on Tyrfounder Farm not far from Cwmbach pit, and he reached the famous 'four foot' seam of coal in June 1842. Further pits quickly sprang up in the area. In 1843 Powell sank nearby Upper Duffryn, whilst the same year William Thomas sunk a pit at

Lletty Shenkin, high on the hillside overlooking Duffryn. Also the same year David Davis sank Blaengawr Colliery in the valley bed nearer to Aberdare. The following year David Williams sank a pit called High Duffryn at Ynyscynon, also in the Cwmbach area.

Within a few more years pits had been sunk at Wyrfa (Werfa) high on the northern hillside overlooking Cwmbach, at Abergawr just across the bed of the valley from the Duffryn pits, at Bwllfa in the Dare valley, at Bedwlwyn (usually spelt Bedlwyn in later days) in the Aman valley, and at Mountain Ash.

A further ironworks was started by Crawshay Bailey at Aberaman in 1845. His name figures prominently in the early railway history of the valley. In March of the same year Bailey sank Aberaman Colliery adjacent to the ironworks. In the early years the coal raised was chiefly for use in the ironworks, and it was not until many years afterwards that Aberaman coal joined the rapidly growing steam coal export trade from the valley. In 1845 all the collieries, except a few of those sunk by the ironworks companies for their own use, were connected by horse-drawn tramroads to the Aberdare canal, whose traffic trebled from 60,898 tons in 1838 to 159,653 tons in 1848.

Before the latter year, however, effective rail competition had commenced. The Taff Vale Railway (TVR) had completed its line from Cardiff throughout to Merthyr in April 1841, and it was only a question of time and enterprise before it extended into the Aberdare valley. The first moves were made in 1844 when Crawshay Bailey along with the celebrated Merthyr ironmaster John Guest - who was also Managing Director of the TVR - sought powers to construct the Aberdare Railway. Aberaman ironworks, and the Cwmbach area collieries, were close to where the proposed railway would pass, and he could foresee an immense increase in traffic along the TVR line once the Aberdare Railway was constructed. The Bill for the line received the Royal Assent on 31st July, 1845 and its public opening was a year later, on 6th August, 1846.

This six foot casting was placed above one entrance to Crawshay Bailey's ironworks at Aberaman. *Welsh Industrial & Maritime Museum*

Chapter Two

Planning the Railway

By 1844 the method of transporting coal from the increasing number of pits in the Aberdare valley was causing considerable concern. Already some 10 pits were working, or in process of sinking, and it was obvious that the canal would soon be unable to cope; the lenght of time involved in getting the coal to Cardiff was also considerable. In the neighbouring Taff valley the Glamorganshire canal had already been challenged by a far more efficient method of transporting minerals, the railway. When the Taff Vale Railway had opened throughout from Merthyr to Cardiff in 1841 iron products were carried from the ironworks to Cardiff in three hours, whereas previously it had taken three days by canal.

So the ironmasters and colliery proprietors got together to discuss the problem and appointed a Mr David Jones to make a survey for a railway which would connect with the TVR near the foot of its main incline at Navigation (now Abercynon), and pass through the valley to terminate near the Gadlys Iron Works at Aberdare. Mr Jones started his survey on 17th August, 1844 and this was completed, plans made, and the whole checked by Mr E. Scott Barber, another Civil engineer, in time for a Bill to be prepared and deposited at Parliament in November.

The first the public knew of the matter was a formal notice in the *Cardiff and Merthyr Guardian* dated 28th November, 1844 which stated:

> Notice is hereby given that application is intended to be made to Parliament, in the next Session, for an Act to authorise the construction of a railway to commence by a junction with the Taff Vale Railway at, or near, a place or farm called Ynys Meyrick within the Parish of Llanwonno and to terminate at, or near, a certain Tram Road leading from the Hirwain Iron Works to the Aberdare Canal, on Gadlys Ucha Farm, in the Parish of Aberdare.

Two branches were intended, one from, or near, Aberaman to Cwm Bach Colliery, the second also from near Aberaman Farm to a farm called Bedlwyn, the latter obviously to serve a small colliery near Bedlwyn Farm. Both branches would be solely within the Parish of Aberdare.

The Aberdare canal proprietors were obviously aware of the proposal to construct a railway as on 11th September, and again on 20th December, they held special meetings with a single item on the agenda: To take into consideration the propriety of reducing the Rates of Tonnage and, if agreed upon, to reduce them accordingly.'

During the progress of the Bill through its Committee stages, Thomas Powell objected to the proposed charges for carrying coal, and insisted on the right to use his own engine on the line. His objection was overruled on the grounds that , as the Aberdare was to be a single line railway, it would be dangerous to allow him to do so, but it was agreed that the charges should be reduced so that 'they be no more than that charged by the Pontypool Railway, which Mr Powell used to transport his Monmouthshire coal'. (The railway referred to was the Monmouthshire Railway and Canal Company.)

The Aberdare Railway received its Act of Incorporation on 31st July, 1845. One branch was dropped from the Bill, the branch from Aberaman to Bedlwyn. Mr Crawshay Bailey, one of the two principal promoters of the line, had started the iron works at Aberaman, and decided to construct the branch privately as far as his works, which he was entitled to do as he owned all the land between the proposed railway and the works. On part of the remainder of the originally proposed branch, between the iron works and Bedlwyn, a tramroad already existed, between quarries at Aberaman and the colliery; but how the output of the colliery, probably small, went away is not clear.

Crawshay Bailey became treasurer of the Aberdare Railway, the other principal promoter, John Guest becoming Chairman. Guest was already Chairman of the TVR and Crawshay Bailey lost no time in getting on the Board of that company also, as the Act authorised the leasing of the Aberdare Railway to the TVR, subject to the approval of three-fifths of the proprietors but, as he explained many years later, he had intended to build the railway on his own.

By 16th September the company was inviting tenders for 500 tons of rail, to Grand Junction Railway pattern, 200 tons of chairs and 10,000 sleepers. The railway almost faithfully followed the south bank of the River Cynon throughout the valley, and as the Aberdare canal had been cut on the other side of the river, it did not, at least initially, interfere with it in any way. By following the river bank no great engineering works were required, although by also following the bends in the river too closely trouble did arise fairly quickly, as the severe curvature of the line at a point east of Mountain Ash meant a speed restriction of 4 mph and difficulty in hauling 100-wagon trains, which later became quite normal practice.

The work had hardly started when the Aberdare Company suggested to the TVR that they should absorb the Aberdare undertaking, but at the TVR Board meeting held 29th October, 1845 the Secretary was ordered to reply that 'the Board regretted that they do not see their way to entertain the suggestion'. Hence the Aberdare Company continued construction on its own.

It was obvious that a cheaply constructed railway was envisaged, as the estimated cost per mile was just over £4,000 whereas the TVR had cost almost £20,000 per mile. However, no tunnels or viaducts were required, and very few bridges, whilst the gradient did not exceed 1 in 240 at any part of the line. Work was completed with unusual speed, and on 22nd June, 1846 the first engine on the line, which had been engaged on ballasting from 9th May passed over the line throughout to Aberdare. Although not specified in the report this must have been the 4-2-0 *Columbia*, one of the American Norris-built engines for the Birmingham and Gloucester Railway. At the Directors' Meeting held at the castle Hotel, Merthyr, on 7th January, 1846, the company's Secretary and the Engineer had been instructed to proceed to either Gloucester or Birmingham and use their best judgement in purchasing one of the Norris engines. At the same meeting a heavy 0-6-0 mineral engine was authorised to be purchased from Messrs Hawthorn, of Newcastle (at a Meeting on 14th January, 1846 a resolution was passed that Sir John Guest should order a further engine from Hawthorns of Newcastle.)

The report that mentioned the first engine on the line also gave some details of the permanent way. It stated that the rails were of 75 lb. yard quality, each 16 ft long, and joint chairs were 28 lb. each. Intermediate chairs were 22 lb. each, and larch sleepers had been laid at approximately one yard intervals. Those under the rail joints were of 10 in. x 5 in. section, intermediate sleepers having a 9 in. x 4½ in. section. Points to Fox's improved patent pattern had been used. No deviation had taken place from the Parliamentary Plans, and the formation had been made for double track if found to be needed at a later date. On one section 1,000 yards of retaining wall against the river had been erected, but the total cost for the 10 miles of track, including the Cwmbach branch and sidings, was not expected to exceed £50,000. Two stations only were originally constructed, one at Aberdare itself, and the other at Mountain Ash, although two others were contemplated.

Snags in the layout were, however, already becoming evident. One correspondent in a letter to the *Cardiff and Merthyr Guardian*, dated 30th May, 1846, pointed out that several collieries were opening out to the north of the Aberdare canal, but these could not communicate with the railway, as there was no method of crossing the canal. Coal from these collieries would have to be conveyed by local tram road to the canal, and thence by barge to Cardiff.

Nevertheless on 28th July, 1846 Mr George Fisher, the TVR's general superintendent, reported to his Board that the rails to Aberdare were complete, and requested instructions as to the use of TVR wagons on the line. The Aberdare's Company Secretary, Captain Lewes, had proposed that TVR wagons be used on the line with a payment of 1/8d. per ton/mile beyond the junction at Navigation. Captain Lewes also proposed that through rates be established to/from Cardiff, and intimated that his company 'were determined to force their way down the TVR line with their own engines'. Fisher pointed out that whilst the Aberdare Company were unlikely to try this out for a while as they had still not received their mineral engine, it would cause anxiety and risk for two parties to work engines on the TVR main line. He mentioned that with a fully loaded train and unfavourable weather conditions it was impossible to stop a down train in less than half a mile, and in certain places the driver could not see more than 150 yards before him on account of the severity of the curves.

An agreement was reached between the respective Boards whereby the Aberdare Railway would use TVR wagons and hand over the trains to that company at the junction. Traffic to/from the branch would be charged two-thirds of the Cardiff to Merthyr rates between Cardiff and Navigation. The Aberdare Company's passenger trains would terminate at the junction, where a separate booking office for the company would be set up. However, in fact on 27th July the TVR agreed to allow Aberdare Railway carriages to run through to Cardiff, and to allow booking from intermediate stations. In November the *Cardiff & Merthyr Guardian* announced that both 1st and 3rd class carriages were now lit with 'a splendid roof lamp', , and was glad that the latter were included. From a BoT report of 8th August it seems the thirds were better than on some lines, being 'seated, covered, and capable of being closed; they have glass windows at the sides'.

Later in July Captain Codrington, Assistant Inspector of Railways, examined the Aberdare line and expressed his intention of reporting it most favourably to the Board of Trade. All was now set for the grand ceremonial opening, fixed to take place on 5th August, 1846, with the public opening the following day. An advertisement appeared in the Cardiff paper on Saturday 1st August, 1846, which stated:

> The railway will be open to the public on Thursday 6th August. The trains will run to and fro from Aberdare to the Navigation Station [official name Navigation House] of the Taff Vale Railway, in conjunction with that company's ordinary trains, and passengers will be booked through to all stations.

Single fares from Aberdare to Navigation would be 1s. 4d. First Class, 1s. Second Class and 8d. Third Class. A special train would also run on the opening day, leaving Aberdare at 8 am and would connect with special trains on the TVR at both Cardiff and Merthyr.

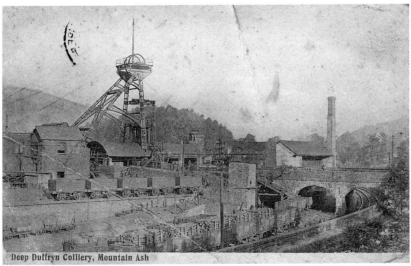

Deep Duffryn Colliery, Mountain Ash

Deep Duffryn Colliery about 1905, showing the bridge over the GWR carrying the TVR branch to George Pit; photograph taken from Duffryn Lock on the Aberdare Canal.
R.W. Kidner Collection

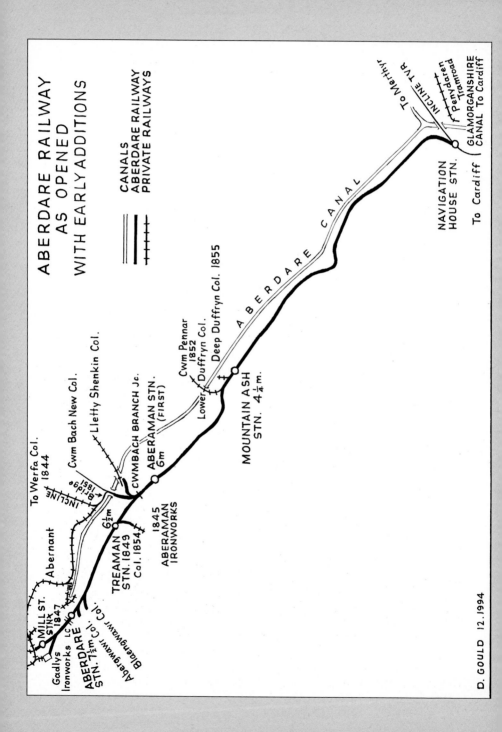

ABERDARE RAILWAY
AS OPENED
WITH EARLY ADDITIONS

CANALS
ABERDARE RAILWAY
PRIVATE RAILWAYS

D. GOULD 12.1994

Chapter Three

The Line Opened and Working

At last the day for the ceremonial opening arrived, although the previous Saturday had been a tragic one for Aberdare as a serious explosion at Duffryn Colliery had cost no less than 28 lives. Even so, on Wednesday 5th August, special trains were run for the benefit of the Directors and their friends to open the line. In the words of the *Cardiff and Merthyr Guardian*:

> From most of the principal houses in Aberdare, and from all the prominent points of the place, flags and banners floated in the breeze and the inhabitants were all neatly decked in their holiday attire. At an early hour in the morning a train, gaily decorated with various colours, evergreens etc., and accompanied by a band of music, left the village and proceeded to Navigation House Station where it met the Up Cardiff train in which was a numerous party consisting of the Directors, their friends, and other notables. The return train to Aberdare was saluted at various places along the line with the firing of cannons and the cheers of the people.

On arrival at Aberdare the Directors, preceded by the band, walked from the station to the Boot Inn, where the Annual General Meeting was then held. In the early afternoon the train returned to Navigation to meet several more dignitaries from Cardiff, and once again made its way back to Aberdare where a celebration champagne dinner was held at the Boot Inn at four o'clock. Those present included just about everyone of note connected with the Taff Vale and Aberdare Railways, the local iron works and the collieries. The principal guest was the Dean of Llandaff; Sir John Guest as Chairman of both the TVR and Aberdare Railway, was well to the fore, and amongst other TVR dignitaries was Walter Coffin (Vice Chairman) and, of course, George Fisher, Crawshay Bailey, Captain Lewes, and the other Aberdare Railway Directors were there along with such famous names in the iron and coal industries as Thomas Powell, Mathew and Thomas Wayne of Gadlys, David Davis, and Mrs Lucy Thomas, who was an early coal prospector in the Merthyr Valley and sometimes referred to as 'the mother of coal trade in South Wales'.

Thomas Powell said he proposed to send 200 tons of coal a day down the line within a month, and 500 tons a day within a year. (In actual fact he started by sending his first 100 tons to Cardiff the following day.) Mrs Lucy Thomas said she would be sending down 300 tons a day within the year, and Messrs Powell and Protheroe would send 300/400 tons a day, David Williams promised 200/300 tons a day, and David Davis a further 300 tons. Everyone was happy: the railway proprietors could foresee a handsome return from their investment, the TVR could see an era of immense expansion of its own trade, and the coal owners could expect quick deliveries to Cardiff.

The public passenger service started on the following day, as arranged; three trains on weekdays and two on Sundays. The Taff Vale altered its main line service so that connections for Cardiff, Merthyr and Aberdare could be

D.G. 12.1994

YSGUBORWEN
Thomas & Joseph 1849

BLAENANT
Aberdare Iron Co. 1852

WERFA
J. Nixon 1844

ABERDARE STN.

CWMBACH
T. Wayne 1837

UPPER DUFFRYN
T. Powell 1843

LLETTY SHENKIN
W. Thomas 1843

TIRFOUNDER
(Old Duffryn)
T. Powell 1840

MIDDLE DUFFRYN
T. Powell 1850

LOWER DUFFRYN
(Cwm Pennar)
T. Powell 1850

DEEP DUFFRYN
D. Williams 1850

NAVIGATION
J. Nixon 1853

MOUNTAIN ASH STN.

GADLYS
Wayne & Co.

BLAENGWAWR
David Davis 1843

ABERGWAWR
T. Powell 1843

TRE-AMAN
D. Williams 1854

CWMNEOL
J. Carr 1854

ABERAMAN
C. Bailey 1845

CWM AMAN
Shepherd & Evans 1849

FFORCHAMAN
Protheroe 1854

BEDW-LWYN
Shepherd & Evans 1843

PENRHIEW LECH
(Merthyr Dare)
D. Williams 1851

TROEDRHIEW LECH
(Cwm Dare)
T. Powell 1851

EARLY COLLIERIES
IN THE ABERDARE VALLEY

With the exception of Merthyr Dare and
Cwm Dare (as later named) all these
sent coal down the Aberdare Railway

made at Navigation House. It is probable that some minor alteration was made to enable three trains to stand together if required, though the Aberdare Railway had its own station just north of the junction. The passenger engine was turned for each trip, but it seems that it must have used the TVR table at Navigation at first, since an Aberdare Railway Board Minute of 15th September, 1852 recommends 'that a turntable for engine and tender be erected on the Aberdare Branch'. The 4-2-0 *Columbia* was working all passenger trains. The 0-6-0 engine worked goods trains through to Cardiff, the TVR Board having agreed on 8th September, 1846 to allow this facility. The fact that the TVR itself did not have too many engines no doubt weighed against an opinion expressed that there was a danger involved in having engines of two companies on one line of rails.

The goods engine arrived on the Aberdare Railway on 8th July. At that time the Taff Vale and Aberdare Railways were in complete isolation from any other railway, and engines, carriages etc. had to be delivered to Cardiff by sea, the TVR having its own little Dock cut in the east bank of the Glamorgan Canal near the TVR terminus. This was the origin of the TVR's West Yard Locomotive Works in Cardiff's dockland, the works gradually being built adjacent to the Little Dock.

The new engine, of 0-6-0 tender type, and fitted with 16 in. diameter inside cylinders was named *Aberaman*. Its success caused the TVR to make 16 in. diameter cylinders standard for mineral engines for many years afterwards.

As the working of the Aberdare line was so tied up with that of the TVR the Directors of the two companies met on 25th November, 1846 and formed an agreement for the leasing of the Aberdare Railway by the TVR. With Sir John Guest and Crawshay Bailey on the Taff Board as well as being principal Directors of the Aberdare Railway, they were able to sit on both sides of the fence. The agreement reached was certainly favourable to the Aberdare Company, and was obviously based on traffic potential (which in the event was fully justified) rather than on the comparatively small amount of traffic that had already passed down the line to the TVR. The basis of the lease agreement was that the TVR would work the line and pay the Aberdare proprietors 7 per cent for the first year, 8 per cent for the second year, 9 per cent for the third year and 10 per cent for the fourth and all subsequent years.

Special meetings of the proprietors of both companies were held at the White Lion Hotel, Bristol, on 15th December, 1846, to consider the agreement. The Aberdare Railway held its meeting first, at 12 noon, and naturally the agreement was approved with scarcely a voice of dissent. The Taff Vale meeting did not go so smoothly and, whilst the Directors received the three-fifths majority in favour, it was not before many angry speeches had been made from the floor. Several shareholders thought the terms far too generous to the Aberdare Company, and others thought it best to defer the matter for a year or two and see how trade developed in the meantime. It took the Chairman all his powers of persuasion to convince the shareholders of the rosy future that lay ahead, but what proved to be the turning point was when he intimated that if the TVR did not take over the working of the line, it was fairly certain that the

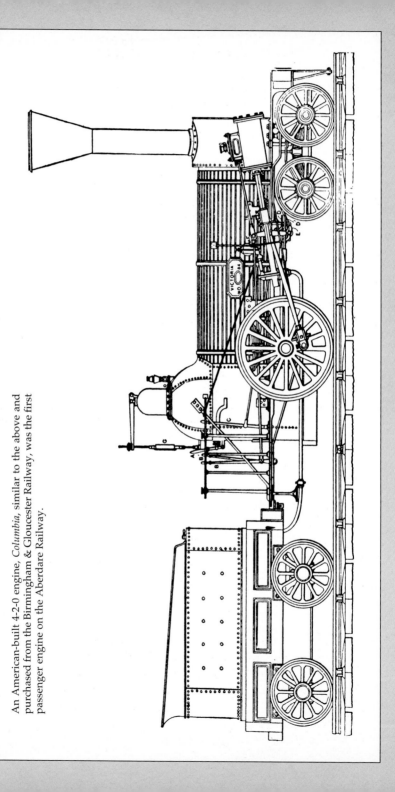

An American-built 4-2-0 engine, *Columbia*, similar to the above and purchased from the Birmingham & Gloucester Railway, was the first passenger engine on the Aberdare Railway.

newly formed Vale of Neath Railway, with GWR backing, would do so. The lease came into effect as from 1st January, 1847, and was later ratified by Act of Parliament dated 30th June, 1848. A further agreement between the respective Boards dated 1st September, 1849 extended the lease from its original 21 years to 999 years; that agreement was backdated to become effective on 1st January, 1849.

However, back to the original TVR General Meeting to discuss the lease; a Mr Hall, one of the TVR shareholders, spoke very unfavourably of the curves and gradients on the Aberdare line which, he said, were calculated to cause great wear and tear on the locomotive engines. He declared that on no line in the kingdom were the curves so bad, and he had recently been told that 'the bearings of the beautiful new engine, bought in September, were already gone to destruction'. Mr David Jones, Engineer of the Aberdare Railway thought it necessary to publicly reply to the charges and, in a letter to the *Cardiff and Merthyr Guardian* dated 22nd December, 1846 stated:

The railway commences from the junction (Navigation) for the first 3 miles 60 chains at a gradient of 1 in 240, followed by a gradient of 1 in 660 for the next 1 mile 20 chains, and at 1 in 360 for the remaining 2 miles 10 chains. Regarding the engine *Aberaman* I at once declare that the bearings of no engine wears more uniformly than the bearings of this engine on the Aberdare line. A better engine, of the size, is not on any railway in the kingdom.

When the TVR took over the working of the railway on 1st January, 1847 two further stations were in course of erection, one at Aberdare Mill Street, nearly a mile north-west of Aberdare station, close to where the Hirwain-Aberdare canal tram road crossed over the Cynon River; the other station was at Aberaman, between the junction for the Cwmbach branch and the junction to Crawshaw Bailey's private branch to Aberaman. Both stations appear to have been created more for Bailey's private benefit than that of the general public, although housing was rapidly developing in the Mill Street area, but there was no public roadway to the station. However Bailey had a private siding at Mill street, where limestone from Penderyn, via the tram road, was loaded into rail wagons for his Aberaman Ironworks. The station most useful for him in this respect. The Aberaman station was much more a private affair, there being neither public road nor footpath to it. A private lane from Bailey's residence, at Aberaman, led to the station which, nevertheless, opened as a public station. Workmen from the Cwmbach area used it, although they had to trespass along the Cwmbach branch, and then a short distance along the main line, to reach it. Workmen at the Aberaman Ironworks, or at the collieries near the mouth of the Aman Valley used to cut across the fields to the station, although Bailey did his best to put a stop to that.

No public announcement of the opening of either station appeared in the press, nor are recorded in TVR minutes, but both appeared in a press advertisement of local train services for 22nd May, 1847, and this was probably the opening date, as it is known that neither were open the previous month. The two stations did not appear in Bradshaw's Timetable for a considerable time, but did appear in timetables in the local press from that date onwards.

The first official changes arising from the working of the line by the TVR came on 19th February, 1847 when the Board ordered that 'as soon as practicable the Superintendent to arrange for all the Carpenters and Mechanics at Aberdare to be removed to Cardiff'. At the same meeting the Aberdare line was ordered to be accurately measured and marked off with ¼ mile posts.

In January the traders at Aberdare had written to the TVR requesting that their goods be delivered from the railway, as happened at Merthyr. At that time most of their goods were delivered by canal and transferred at Canal Head to the tram road, from which they had to be collected at a central point. George Fisher suggested that the goods should be conveyed by rail and delivered within a ½ mile radius of the station. He submitted that two horses, one light cart and one trolley was all that was necessary. One horse with the cart would be able to carry out most of the deliveries, the other horse would be employed in the station yard, except when required for the delivery of heavy goods.

At the same time Fisher notified the Board that he had prepared, and issued, rules and Regulations for working the Aberdare branch. He mentioned that since the opening of the line, although the passenger trains had worked to timetable, there had been no fixed times for the goods and coal trains, these being run entirely at the convenience of the Aberdare Company.

Whilst *Columbia* continued with the passenger service, Taff Vale mineral engines worked through to the Aberdare valley on the coal trains, to assist the overworked *Aberaman*. The Aberdare Company had erected two small wooden sheds immediately west of the road level crossing at Aberdare, one to house each engine. After the TVR took control *Aberaman* was transferred to the Taff engine shed at Cardiff Docks, as the TVR custom at that time was that all goods and mineral trains started the day from Cardiff, worked up the valley and returned to Cardiff in the afternoon or evening. The *Columbia* being a passenger engine, remained at Aberdare and plied daily between Mill Street and Navigation House.

Navigation House station was a short distance north of the present Abercynon station and almost at the foot of the 1 in 20 rope-worked incline on the main line to Merthyr. Fisher submitted that a new station was required. He stated that at the point where the down passenger train left the rope there was only 20 feet between the TVR and Aberdare lines. There was insufficient room to build a new station and dwelling house between the tracks, but suggested a platform with booking office and waiting rooms could be accommodated. He estimated the cost of same as £377 5s. 0d. However the Directors did not agree and on 23rd March, 1848 ordered that 'the wooden shed at Navigation be removed to the tongue of land between the Taff and Aberdare Railways near their junction'. This meant moving the station somewhat nearer to the site of the present Abercynon station.

One further station was erected on the Aberdare line in 1848. This was Treaman, about ½ mile west of Aberaman station, where housing development was taking place for the men employed at the Aberaman Iron Works and two nearby collieries. This probably relieved Crawshay Bailey also, as he could now regard Aberaman even more as a private station. The distance of the stations from Navigation House, as given in Bradshaw's Timetables, were Mountain Ash (4¼ miles), Aberaman (6 miles), Treaman (6½ miles), Aberdare (7½ miles) and Mill Street (8½ miles). Again no public announcement was made of the opening of Treaman station, but it was authorised by the Board on 26th September, 1848, was stated in correspondence to be under erection on 5th October, and opened a few days alter. Being a single line railway the provision of an intermediate station did not involve much expense, a solitary platform with a wooden booking office cum waiting room was all that was provided.

The Aberdare Railway was first fully detailed in Fisher's annual report to his Directors at the close of 1849. He reported that the main line from Navigation to Mill Street terminus was 8 miles 8½ chains in length, and the Cwmbach branch 60 chains long. At Navigation the Aberdare Company had 51 chains of sidings and at Mountain Ash there was a short siding where wagons were loaded with material from a nearby quarry. Leading from the Cwmbach branch was a further 34½ chain siding for Lletty Shenkin Colliery, although this could not connect to the colliery until agreement had been reached with the canal company regarding construction of a bridge over the canal.

Also from the Cwmbach branch were two short sidings, one to Lower Duffryn Colliery (known after 1850 as Old Duffryn), the other to Upper Duffryn Colliery. The branch continued for a short distance to serve Cwmbach and Ynyscynon (High Duffryn) collieries. All four pits lay between the canal and the River Cynon, well within a distance of half a mile, and could thus be served by the railway as the branch crossed the river immediately before entering the colliery area.

No mention was made of the Aberaman branch which had been privately constructed by Crawshay Bailey, and the next siding was at Treaman station. Further towards Aberdare was a 14 chain-long siding to Abergwawr Colliery, and a short spur into the gas works where, Fisher stated, only one wagon of coal was delivered weekly.

Just before Aberdare station was a 10 chain siding serving Blaengwawr Colliery, and at the station itself were some ¾ of a mile of sidings. Between the station and Mill Street were sidings for the Gadlys Ironworks with a separate siding to that company's colliery, and at the terminus were three further short sidings. The lengths of sidings quoted by Fisher were, naturally, the extent which the TVR maintained; in most cases these were extended by the trader to suit his own convenience, and the extension maintained by him, or at his own expense.

In those days it was not the practice to protect the junction of a siding with the main line, other than by a normal signal. These were of the standard disc and crossbar pattern from the opening of the line, as on the TVR. This led to a serious tragedy at the town level crossing at Aberdare on Monday 30th June, 1851. The Gadlys Iron Company's siding was some 500 yards to the west of the crossing gates, and on an inclination of 1 in 112. The practice of the Gadlys Company was to load wagons with iron products on this section, and, when full, an empty wagon was moved into position, bumping the loaded wagon forward towards the main line. Just before reaching the main line the brakes were applied. At 4 pm on that particular sunny afternoon the brakes of one loaded wagon either failed or were not properly applied, and the wagon careered on to the main line and sped towards the crossing gates 'just as a great concourse of people were parading across accompanied by the local brass band'. The gradient between the siding and the crossing gates was 1 in 182, falling towards the crossing, and because of the music few saw, or heard, the wagon approaching. It crashed through the gates killing four women instantly and badly injuring three other people.

Fisher immediately had safety points fitted on the main line to protect the crossing but, as he reported, this did not entirely remedy the matter as a similar breakaway could happen when a passenger or mineral train was proceeding between the crossing and Mill Street. Fisher had complained of similar incidents, fortunately without such disastrous results, from other sidings and particularly from Crawshay Bailey's branch, and on 24th July, 1851 the Board ordered safety switches to be fitted on all new private branches, also on all existing ones within seven days of notice being given. Unfortunately the colliery owners and iron masters of the day were very powerful men and many failed to comply, and as late as 18th January, 1854 Fisher reminded his Directors that neither the Gadlys Company or Crawshay Bailey had taken the slightest notice of the instruction.

The small 6- and 8-ton coal wagons gave way to 10-ton ones before the end of the century; however this example still has 'dumb' buffers and wooden brake-blocks.   *Lens of Sutton*

Chapter Four

Early Problems Overcome

The early days of the railway were full of incidents that make strange reading in these modern times, several due to the extremely poor passenger trains of three trains each way only per day. On 23rd July, 1849 Crawshay Bailey wrote to Fisher asking him to send an engine up to Aberaman to pick him up to attend a Director's meeting, as 'he did not have time to wait four hours in Cardiff doing nothing'. On 21st December, 1847 J. Bruce Pryce complained that the previous day he was waiting at Mountain Ash station for the last train down to Navigation House and thence on to Cardiff; the train with *Columbia* at the head limped into Mountain Ash 10 minutes late, whereupon he was informed that the fire bars had fallen out between Aberaman and Mountain Ash, and another engine would have to be sent for from Navigation. By the time he eventually reached the junction the Cardiff train had long since gone, but after a two hour wait he was taken to Cardiff by the last down coal train. His main complaint was not that he was so badly delayed and had to complete his journey in a coal train, but that if the *Columbia* had been property examined at Aberdare it would have been impossible for the bars to have been burnt through in the three mile journey to Mountain Ash.

On 2nd February, 1847 a quarry man, Morgan Morgan of Duffryn, was permitted to load stone wagons on the main line, near Mountain Ash, after the last mineral train had gone, and the *Aberaman* engine presumed safely back in shed. The driver, however, decided to make one more trip down to Navigation and back, and not having informed Morgan Morgan, in fact he only told a platelayer working further up the line towards Aberdare, his engine crashed into the stone wagons, completely demolishing one and badly damaging the others.

On 29th July, 1847 a train of empties arrived at Cwmbach Junction for the branch, for which the point should have been set. Unfortunately the policeman at the junction, one Mr Petty, was fast asleep in his cabin, and had set the signal for the branch but not the points, and the train continued up the main line. Although this only meant reversal - and waking Mr Petty up doubtless - it does illustrate railway working at the time. One can feel sympathy for the unfortunate policeman, tiredness must have been prevalent in those days of very long working hours. This particular man was on duty from the first mineral train in the morning until the last had gone for the night, and besides looking after the Cwmbach Junction, he also had to attend to the points and signals at the junction with Crawshay Bailey's Aberaman branch some ¼ mile westwards, and look after and issue tickets at Aberaman station, which lay between the two junctions.

As late as 1860 prominent personalities were still asking the TVR for passes to travel by coal trains as the passenger service was so inadequate, one such request on 28th June, 1860, from a Mr John Ryle, ending with the phrase, 'my horse would be hardly be able to do the distance'.

Besides tiredness, drunkenness by railway employees was also a source of worry to the authorities. Several engine drivers were reported as being 'drunk in charge' in the very early days, and the driver of the *Columbia*, one John Jenkins, and his fireman were no exceptions. In 1849, however, after having killed several horses, cows and bulls (or steers as he preferred to call them) on his numerous trips between Aberdare and Navigation, John Jenkins had had enough, and quit his job.

Although a 'rough diamond' of his day, his letter of resignation was the height of correctness, and certainly better than many far more educated people in a similar position could frame today. Dated 6th March, 1849, and addressed to George Fisher Esquire, superintendent of the Taff Vale Railway, he wrote:

Sir,
I beg leave to give you notice that I will leave the situation of engine Driver on the Aberdare branch at the expiration of a fortnight from this day.
Yours obediently,

JOHN JENKINS.

It was at much the same time that Navigation House station was re-named Aberdare Junction. As usual no public announcement was made of the change, but it was definitely in the early summer of 1849, and probably when the TVR passenger timetable was completely revised as from Tuesday 1st May, 1849. Despite the new name the station continued to be generally known as Navigation for several years; although previously officially called Navigation House, it was seldom called other than Navigation even in official correspondence. George Fisher was still calling it Navigation in some of his reports to his Directors as late as 1857.

During 1849 the Taff carried 223,057 tons of minerals, practically all coal, down the Aberdare Valley, compared with 15,409 tons from the opening to 31st December, 1846, and 88,117 tons during 1847. However there were still several collieries not connected to the railway, particularly those to the north of the canal, and the threat of competition from the approaching Vale of Neath Railway, which would pass on the hillside fairly close to these collieries spurred the TVR into taking some positive action to gain access across the canal.

Of the collieries involved there were Lletty Shenkin, sunk by William Thomas in 1843, Werfa (Wyrfa) sunk by John Nixon in 1844, and the coal levels being worked by Mr Fothergill close to his iron works at Abernant. These collieries and coal levels were all on the hillside to the north-east of the canal, roughly in the area between Aberdare and Cwmbach, and already having to work their traffic by rope worked inclines between the canal and colliery. To connect with the railway, bridges were needed and up till that time the canal company had, naturally, resisted all efforts made by the TVR to establish them. When the dispute resulted in an inquiry, and later in court action, the TVR had to sit on the touch line as the legal dispute was between the landowners concerned and the canal company.

The inquiry was held at the Boot Inn, Aberdare, on 12th February, 1849, before Commissioners established under the provisions of the Aberdare Canal Company's Act of Parliament. The test case was between the Trustees of Lord Bute, as landowners, and the canal company as to the right of the trustees to build a bridge across the canal to open a communication with the Aberdare Railway. It was stated that the trustees were owners of the land through which the canal was cut, and also owners of Cwmbach farm and other lands on both sides of the canal. They also owned land to the north-east which was sub-let to Mr Nixon, and upon which he had established his Wyrfa colliery. There was already a tram road, on an inclined plane, leading down from the colliery to the canal bank at Cwmbach, but in order to carry coal to the Aberdare Railway, a bridge over the canal was required.

George Fisher outlined the proposed bridge, saying it would have a clear way of 20 ft between the abutments, which was ample for the water way and towing path. The headway at the centre of the bridge would be 8 ft, and at each side 7 ft 4 in. In his opinion that would decidedly not interfere with navigation on the canal.

The canal company relied on the usual clause in their Act that bridges should not be constructed for the purpose of diverting traffic from the canal. Nevertheless, the Commissioners granted permission for the bridge to be erected, also a second bridge applied for by Messrs Wayne and Company, who worked collieries on the north side of the canal near Cwmbach.

This was not the end of the matter, however, and the canal company delayed the bridge building for nearly two years by issuing a Writ of Certiorari, claiming that the inquiry had not been properly called, that the Commissioners were biased towards the railway, and that some of them were financially interested. Their appeal was heard in a Court of the Queen bench on 26th January, 1850 and upheld on the technical issue that the inquiry had not been called properly. A second inquiry was not held until Tuesday 5th November, 1850, and on this occasion it was made sure that official notification was correctly made in local newspapers. As before, the commissioners gave their findings in favour of the applicants for the bridges and these were put up early in 1851.

The bridge for the Werfa traffic was the first completed and the tram road to the colliery was converted to normal 4 ft 8½ in. gauge rail track, connecting to the Cwmbach branch of the TVR. As the colliery was high up on the hillside, about one mile from the canal bridge, the rope-worked incline had to be retained, and by 1853 Fisher was complaining of the excessive wear and tear on TVR wagons using the incline.

The canal company did not resist a bridge being built to cater for the Lletty Shenkin traffic. This was erected by the colliery owner, who also established a second small colliery at the lower end of his inclined plane, sited between the canal and the River Cynon. This was mainly a transfer point, the coal being brought down the incline between Lletty Shenkin Upper and Lower Collieries by tram road wagons, and transferred to rail wagons at the Lower Colliery. A basin from the canal was adjacent to this colliery, hence shipment could be made by canal if desired. The Lletty Shenkin branch left the Cwmbach branch almost immediately after leaving Cwmbach Junction, and crossed the River Cynon by a separate bridge a few yards east of the bridge carrying the Cwmbach branch over the river. Five years later (in 1856) when the new Aberdare Valley Railway extended the broad gauge Vale of Neath line eastwards along the valley to the Duffryn area, the broad gauge rails were also laid between the river and the canal, necessitating two rail level crossings within a few yards of each other. The signal box between them carried the imposing name 'Cwmbach and Lletty Shenkin Crossing Signal Box'.

Next came the question of rail connection to the Aberdare Iron Company and, at first, Fisher was inclined to build a separate branch to the Abernant Iron works and nearby coal levels. On 11th November, 1851 he proposed a branch from the main line near Blaengawr, which would swing off northwards at an inclination of 1 in 140, and by bridges pass over the River Cynon, the Aberdare Coal Company's tram road, and finally over the Parish Road. Just beyond the road the branch would have ended, the continuation to the works being by tram road 67 chains long, the first half of which would have been on an inclined plane 1 of in 10. A second tramroad eastwards from the same junction would have served the coal levels. Mr Fothergill, the Abernant ironmaster, did not agree; he wanted railway wagons to carry his traffic direct, and not have the delay necessary transhipping loads between the tram road and railway. He therefore constructed his own standard gauge private branch from the Iron works to connect with the TVR at the west end of the Cwmbach branch. Although involving some stiff gradients, this branch was worked by the Abernant Company's own engines.

Further collieries were being sunk in several areas at the time. Near the mouth of the Dare Valley, immediately south of Aberdare itself, David Williams started sinking Merthyr Dare Colliery (then called Penrhiw Llech) in 1851, and about the same time Thomas Powell started sinking Cwmdare Colliery nearby, then Troedrhiw Lech but better known as Powell's Pit. Fisher was asked to prepare a scheme for a branch to the two pits, no easy matter without the nuisance of inclined planes, as both pits involved severe gradients, particularly Mr Williams' which was a little further into the valley, and higher up the mountainside than Mr Powells' pit. He suggested a continuation of the siding to the Gadlys Iron Company's colliery. This he said was 44 chains long at a gradient of 1 in 41, and TVR engines passed over this siding to the colliery three times each day. The continuation to Mr Williams' pit would necessitate a further 76 chains at a gradient of about 1 in 39. Although the line would continue for a further 10 chains or so at the same gradient that, in his opinion, was the extent a locomotive line could be made.

Although the Dare Valley was only about two miles in length, and it was estimated that there was sufficient coal to raise 1,000 tons per day for the next 80 to 100 years, Fisher advised his board that, in his opinion, the future of the valley lay in the manufacture of iron, rather than sending their coal away, as ironstone was on hand, and limestone from the Penderyn Quarry could easily be conveyed to the site by existing Hirwain-Aberdare Tram Road. On his advice the Directors took no further action to construct the branch, particularly as Fisher had stated that he saw no way in which the Vale of Neath could get into the valley without bringing its line down to Aberdare and entering the valley in the Gadlys area. This, he said, would make the distance from pit to port longer to Swansea by the Vale of Neath, than to Cardiff by the Taff Vale and, in any case, it was accepted 'that all minerals should be conveyed in the direction of the water streams of the valleys'.

This was probably Fisher's most erroneous report to his Directors. The Dare Valley never became an iron making centre, but it did develop into one of the greatest coal producing areas in South Wales. Further, the Vale of Neath did get into the valley without going into Aberdare. Fisher must have overlooked that the master, himself, Brunel, was Engineer of the Vale of Neath Railway. Brunel did it by erecting two of his famous wooden viaducts, spanning the valleys and reversing at high level into the Dare Valley; it was a further 15 years before the TVR had access to the wealth of the Dare Valley.

Fisher had enough problems dealing with further pits being sunk, and the Aberdare branch was only part, although admittedly the most important part at the time, of the whole Taff Vale system he had to look after. On 11th April, 1850 he reported on a proposed branch to the new colliery which Mr Powell was opening up in the Aberdare valley. Although a comparatively simple branch, only 41 chains long across the bed of the valley and involving just one bridge over the River Cynon, this branch, or siding, became probably the best known in South wales, as the colliery was the famous Middle Duffryn Colliery and the siding the Middle Duffryn Siding. In few local railway histories will you see the names of Werfa or Lletty Shenkin Collieries, but you will certainly find Middle Duffryn. This somewhat isolated colliery, just over ½ mile east of Powell's Old Duffryn Colliery at Cwmbach - and ½ mile gap made a colliery somewhat isolated in those days - became the mecca of all railways trying to cash in on the wealth of the Aberdare coal trade in the later 1850s and early 1860s.

The siding to Middle Duffryn Colliery was duly laid in 1850 and coal commenced flowing from it to the TVR by the autumn of that year. However, Powell had already commenced sinking another pit in the Cwmpennar area just west of Mountain Ash, whilst David Williams had also commenced sinking Deep Duffryn Colliery in the same area. Although it was expected to be two years (1852) before coal was raised at either pit, Powell proposed that a branch should be put in from the Taff Vale line, immediately west of the road bridge at Mountain Ash, to serve Deep Duffryn Colliery and continued over the canal to his own pit which he called Lower Duffryn. Coal was not won as soon as he expected at either colliery, and in 1851 Mr Williams told Fisher that 'rather than have his coal mixed up with Mr Powell's he would make his own branch'. Deep Duffryn Colliery was almost adjacent to the Taff line, and in August 1853 the Board authorised a separate siding to the colliery, although this was not opened until 1855 when coal was at last won. Meanwhile Powell's siding to Lower Duffryn had been opened in 1853, the Taff Vale constructing the first 26½ chains and the bridge over the Cynon, Powell completing it thence to the colliery. A few years later this private section was extended to a second pit higher on the hillside, necessitating an inclined plane , the two collieries then being known as Cwmpennar Upper and Lower Pits.

To the west of Aberdare Messrs Thomas and Joseph had, in 1849, sunk a pit close to the Llwydcoed Iron Works. This was called Ysguborwen, although two or three different spellings have been found on different documents.   A tramroad with inclined plane served the iron works higher up the hillside, but the proprietors requested a standard gauge siding towards the colliery from the Taff Vale line. This could only be achieved by extending the line beyond the terminus at Mill Street, and immediately beyond that point both the River Cynon and the Aberdare-Hirwain Tram Road curved round to cross the pathway at right angles. There was no urgency for the branch, it usually took at least three years to reach the coal once sinking had commenced, and in the meantime the colliery was served by tram road leading to a siding in the Taff Vale yard at Mill Street.

On 5th February, 1851 Fisher reported that it was not the intention of the colliery proprietors for the branch to go right to the colliery, as the latter was more than a mile from Mill Street and between 800 and 1,000 feet higher than the rail level at that point. Messrs Thomas and Joseph would form an inclined plane down the hillside to a point some 23 chains from Mill Street, and work this by tram road with transhipping to railway wagons at the foot of the incline. The rail branch would extend from Mill Street in one continuous curve northwards at an inclination of about 1 in 60, crossing the newly constructed Vale of Neath line on the level. Fisher estimated the TVR branch would cost £1,781 10s. 0d.

On 13th October, 1851 Messrs Thomas and Joseph intimated that construction of the branch should begin, the TVR to build the bridge over the river and the branch to the foot of the incline. It was finally completed in 1854, several deviations from the originally proposed route being made. The branch, actually 66½ chains long, passed over the River Cynon a few yards after leaving Mill Street, and then immediately passed over the Aberdare-Hirwain Tram Road on the level. As the Taff Vale and Vale of Neath Railways ran parallel to each other only a few yards apart at this point the poor Tram Road, which had been first in the field, had to suffer two rail level crossings, by two separate railway companies, within a fell yards. The branch continued on a northerly curve, but owing to objections by the Vale of Neath Company now passed under their line and across the fields beyond to the foot of the incline leading to the colliery. The branch extended a short way past this point to other coal levels in the area. In later years a new pithead for Ysguborwen was sited almost alongside the branch and this meant the inclined plane could be done away with.

With so many collieries opening, the mineral traffic on the Aberdare line increased at an amazing pace; the 223,000-odd tons taken down in 1849 had increased to 387,127 tons in 1852 and 484,249 tons the following year, and reached 920,558 tons - of which 850,416 tons represented coal - in 1856. Fisher now had other problems connected with the Aberdare line, apart from branches and sidings to new collieries. For one thing the Vale of Neath Railway which, in 1851, had made Aberdare what appeared to be a harmless terminus of its branch, was now opening out into a lucrative coal field. In 1852 it had obtained Parliamentary authorisation to extend into both Dare and Aman valleys, and even into the Aberdare Valley itself as far as Canal Head; by 1855 came similar authorisation to continue eastwards through the valley to Middle Duffryn, covering all the collieries in the Cwmbach area *en route*.

It would appear that the TVR had recognised the threat, for on 5th February, 1851 the Management rejected a request from the Vale of Neath for a joint station in Aberdare. In the event, the V of N secured a larger and better-situated plot for their higher level station.

Fisher was painfully aware of the somewhat poor state of the track, in the light of the rapidly expanding tonnage of coal to be carried, and that it was a single line railway between the Junction and Aberaman Siding. A passing loop at Mountain Ash was recommended by the Board on 15th January, 1851.

On 5th December, 1851 he had reported on the necessity of a second passing loop nearer to Aberdare, and suggested that this should be put down at Treaman station. He reminded the Board that on the four miles above Mountain Ash there were no less than seven branches to collieries, and more were contemplated. At that time there were nine booked coal trains daily on the branch. Despite glowing accounts and congratulations showered on the occasion of the opening of the line just over six years previously, Fisher reported on 12th January, 1853 that,

> On the Aberdare line there is much to be done in replacing defective rails and sleepers. The line was imperfectly put on the peat foundation without ballast, the chairs on the sleepers without felt or any proper fastening, added to which they used the very worst of rails and left incomplete the worst constructed railway in Great Britain.

He concluded his report by saying that there were 17 trains each way daily on the line, and urged the Board to double it without delay. In a further report on 1st February he said that to put the Aberdare Railway in order a second line should be laid, and that should be used as a single line until the original line had been taken up and completely re-laid. To emphasise his other report he added,

> The original line was laid on the formation as they found it, without bottom or top ballast, the chairs put upon the sleepers without felt or proper fastenings, the consequence is the bolt heads have sunk into the bottoms of the sleepers, the chairs are loose upon their beds to such an extent that the chairs and rails frequently move laterally half an inch as trains pass over.

On 11th May, 1853 Fisher complained of the very bad curve that followed the course of the river, some 1½ miles east of Mountain Ash. He suggested that a deviation in the line should be made by building two bridges across the bend of the river, as that would considerably straighten out the curvature. He estimated that the cost of two single line bridges of timber construction, plus the cost of the rails and land to be purchased on the north bank of the river, would be in the region of £1,300, but the curve would be increased from 6½ chains radius to 24 chains radius.

No immediate reaction came from the Board but in his annual report for 1853 Fisher again stated that the Aberdare branch was in bad condition, but that during the last half of the year upwards of 14,000 tons of cinder ballast had been put upon it. Following this report the Board authorised doubling of the branch, and a year later, on 22nd January, 1855, Fisher was able to report that ballasting of most of the branch had been completed, sleepers and rails had been renewed, and that two miles had already been doubled. A Board Meeting on 7th February called for further doubling and for the easing of curves on the line. By 2nd October, 1856 Fisher was able to report that doubling of the branch would be completed by the following Monday, apart from the section around the sharp curve. Finally on 28th January, 1857 he gave his brightest report on the branch saying 'I may state that the Aberdare Branch, as far as the permanent way, is much more perfect than any other portion of the company's line'. Nevertheless, he still stressed the urgency of taking out the severe curve as soon as possible.

It was necessary to obtain Parliamentary authority for the deviation, achieved by the Taff Vale's 1857 Act, dated 17th August, 1857, which authorised two such deviations, the one on the Aberdare branch, between the 18¼ and 18¾ mile posts, and the other a 'railway rounding Aberdare Junction Station' enabling the mineral traffic from the Aberdare branch to avoid the platform road. Tenders for the deviation on the Aberdare branch were received by 9th November, 1858, a Mr J.E. Billups, who secured the contract, starting work on 10th March, 1859. Double line bridges were erected and Fisher reported the work completed and ready for use on 21st February, 1860. As from that date the Aberdare branch was double track from Aberdare Junction to just west of Aberdare station, where it singled to cross the road level crossing and thence to Mill Street.

The tonnage of mineral traffic down the branch exceeded one million tons per annum in 1859, when no less than 1,106,872 tons were carried, but still the boom continued and the following year, after John Nixon had won coal at his famous Navigation Colliery at Mountain Ash, the total jumped to 1,313,087 tons. Passenger traffic had, however, suffered the setback of two station closures in the 1850s. First to go was Mill Street station at Aberdare, which was closed as and from Monday 22nd November, 1852. No reason was given for closure, although numerous complaints had been made of the delays caused at the town level crossing gates due to the number of trains passing over. By terminating at Aberdare station the level crossing was avoided by the passenger trains. Probably the real reason was the increase of mineral traffic from west of the gates, the passenger trains no doubt being considered an inconvenience in that section.

The second station to go was Aberaman, after the last train on Saturday 12th July, 1856. Fisher, who never had any great love for Crawshay Bailey, had suggested closure of the station to his Directors in March 1855, but with Bailey such a powerful force both on the railway and in the valley, the Board, on 3rd April, 1855, deferred a decision on the suggestion. On 3rd April, 1856 Fisher again raised the matter with the Board. He argued that Treaman station was only ½ mile distant from Aberaman, and as there was no public access to the latter, 'it would appear that the station was placed there entirely for Mr Bailey's convenience'. He added that the total receipts at the station 'do little exceed £3 per week'.

No action was taken by the Directors, but the doubling of the Aberdare branch came as en unexpected help to Fisher. On 25th June, 1856 he reported to the Directors that, due to doubling, it had been necessary to demolish Aberaman station, although he had replaced it with a temporary structure. He added that it had come to his notice 'that Mr Bailey will shortly be leaving Aberaman, consequently the station will be of less importance than it is at present'. He asked for a decision whether a new station should be built, or simply a cottage for the policeman at Cwmbach Junction. The Board authorised closure to the public at their meeting held the same day, stipulating that trains would still stop 'to take up, and put down, Mr Bailey when he travels by us'. They also authorised a cottage to be built for the policeman. Probably as a parting shot to Crawshay Bailey, rather than to inform the public, Fisher had an official closure notice inserted in the local paper, which simply stated 'After Saturday July 12th 1856, the station at Aberaman will be discontinued. George Fisher, General Superintendent'.

The doubling of the line resulted in new stations being built at Mountain Ash and Treaman. The station at Aberdare, being the Terminus, remained a single platform, the second line used by the through mineral trains to Mill Street. The new station at Mountain Ash was built on a new site slightly nearer to Navigation Colliery, which was in process of sinking at the time. Fisher submitted plans and estimates for the new station on 15th May, 1856; these were authorised and the station completed by the end of November of the same year.

Treaman station was also renewed on a different site, a short distance from the then existing station, and this enabled both the old single platform stations to be kept in use whilst the new stations were being built. The Inspector for the Board of Trade examined the doubled branch on 23rd December, 1856 but, with a few minor modifications to be carried out, it was not until a further inspection on 24th January, 1857 that authorisation was received for its use by the public; 28th January can be considered as the opening date for the two new stations.

Up to the summer of 1853 the Taff had used the old handwritten tickets for passenger traffic, but on 13th July of that year the Board decided to discontinue the old paper tickets, and adopt Edmondson's card tickets as soon as the necessary arrangements could be made. This led to abuse, particularly between Mountain Ash and Aberdare Junction. On 20th May, 1858 Fisher reported that a ticket to Aberdare Junction taken out by a passenger on the first down train was collected by the guard and returned to Mountain Ash and re-issued to a passenger for the same journey on the midday train. He alleged the practice had been carried out to a very considerable extent, tickets issued by the third, and last, train being returned to Mountain Ash where the date was obliterated and altered to the following day. The station master and one guard were involved in the collusion, and he suggested that in future 'a superior class of man be appointed as Station Masters'.

When the Taff doubled the first section of its main line from Cardiff northwards (commenced in 1845), it adopted the unusual method of running its trains on the right hand road, and not the left road as normal practice. This did not matter much in the early days, but with the approach of the Newport, Abergavenney and Hereford Railway (NA&HR) from the east towards the Aberdare Valley, and a connection with that railway being made at Quaker's Yard at the beginning of January 1858, the Directors - late in 1857 - authorised train working to be altered to the normal method. This meant numerous alterations for Fisher to worry about, and on 10th December he complained that to comply with the instruction he had to alter the position of the brake lever on every wagon the company possessed. Still the alterations were all completed when the NA&HR started using its running powers over the Taff Vale main line between Quaker's Yard and Merthyr, on Tuesday 5th January, 1858.

The most astonishing event in the 1850s was the Taff's closure of Aberdare Junction station to the public from 30th October, 1855 to 1st May, 1856. The trouble started soon after the TVR commenced working the Aberdare line in 1847. On 23rd November of that year Fisher reported that a new Public House (The Junction Inn) which had been built near the (then) Navigation House station, was a dangerous nuisance, as two gates from the Inn opened direct on to the railway. Nothing further is recorded until 5th October, 1853 when authorisation was given for a wall to be built to fence off the Inn from the railway.

This did not apparently solve the trespass problem as on 3rd October, 1855 the Board authorised the suspension of the booking of passengers at the station, and that necessary public notice be given. Unfortunately the public notice in the press merely referred to a number of changes being made to the passenger services, and referred interested parties to handbills available at all stations. Closure, as far as passengers entering or leaving the station were concerned, duly took place after the last train on Saturday 29th October, the public being advised that alternative facilities were available at Incline Top station (1 mile north of Aberdare Junction) or at Newbridge station (now Pontypridd) 3¼ miles south. The amazing thing is that Aberdare Junction still remained the changing station for the Aberdare branch, but access to or from the station was prohibited. Worse still, the down trains from Incline Top station did not connect with the Aberdare branch passenger service, entailing lengthy waits at the 'ghost' station, the only alternative for local people being the long walk down to Newbridge to catch a suitable up connecting train.

Extreme public anger was aroused, and protest meetings were held at both Merthyr and Mountain Ash. Extracts from speeches made at the meeting held at the Temperance Hall, Merthyr on Friday 18th November, 1855 reveal the mood of the people. One speaker said that;

> Mr Hoare had taken the public house at Navigation with the promise that every facility should be given of access to the house by crossing the railway, but after some differences sprung up between Mr Evan Davies (Hoare's Landlord) and George Fisher,

whom all knew to be the incarnation of the Taff Vale Railway . . . Now when individual passions govern public bodies the result is that besides private parties, the public interests are injured also. Measures were taken to cut off all communication with the House. Hoare then took steps to obtain his rights - rights reserved to his Landlord by deed - of having a right of way across the line. Finding that persons still crossed the line to get to the House they stationed a policeman there to prevent them, and then placed long lines of wagons in the way. Even this did not succeed. Now it is a peculiarity of the TVR that when ordinary means to attain their ends fail, they have recourse to violence, and take extraordinary means to attend their ends.

(Here he quoted an earlier case in the Rhondda Valley which resulted in the TVR being prosecuted). He concluded with:

They have now dared to close Navigation station after it has been open for 15 years, they have dared to close a public station to gratify their vengeance against a private party, and they must be made to answer for their act. If one now wishes to go to Mountain Ash, one must either go all the way to Pontypridd, or wait two hours by the train from the Incline.

Others present spoke on similar lines, particularly at the difficulty of getting to Mountain Ash or Aberdare, but the chief target of abuse was, decidedly, George Fisher. It was resolved to take the matter to the bail court in an endeavour to get the station re-opened.

The case was heard before Mr Justice Crompton on 1st December, 1855, the applicants basing their case that the railway did not have the right to close a public station which had been built under parliamentary authority. The TVR defended its action on the grounds of public safety. The judge refused the application saying that 'in his opinion there was no foundation for the "once a station, always a station" argument. The railway company must accommodate according to the convenience of the public and themselves'. At this late stage one wonders how the closure of an important junction station could be regarded as for 'the convenience of the public'. Although this seemed to be the end of the matter Mr Evan Davies sought an injunction, at the Rolls Court, on Saturday 22nd December, 'to restrain the TVR from placing trucks on the line at Navigation, the junction station for the Aberdare Railway, or otherwise obstructing the plaintiff in crossing the railway on the level'. The Taff, again basing its case on public safety, quoting the phenomenal increase of traffic since the railway had been opened, and again the application was refused.

The court cases and the bitter feeling aroused penetrated the hallowed walls of the Taff Board Room and in February 1856 the Board made the following statement:

In consequence of great inconvenience to the railway and of danger to human life, it has been found necessary to suspend the operations of the Navigation station [remember it had been officially re-named Aberdare Junction in May 1849] as one for booking passengers but the Board, feeling very desirous to restore accommodation as quickly as possible, have ordered the erection of a bridge across the River Taff to join the station. This is now in the course of construction and will, it is believed, remove the danger and difficulties existing, and meet all the requirements of the public. Meantime passengers are booked for any station on the line from the Incline Top station, within an easy distance.

The bridge and accompanying footbridge over the railway was duly constructed, and Aberdare Junction station was re-opened to the public as from 1st May, 1856, although the station did not re-appear in local official timetables until 1st July, 1856 (main line) and 17th November, 1856 (Aberdare branch).

Details of this extraordinary occurrence have been given fully as there can be few, if indeed any other, cases where a junction station has been closed to access, although continuing in use as a changing station. One can hardly imagine another case where the public had to walk over three miles to catch a train, to make a connection with a branch train waiting at a closed station right outside their doorstep. Still such was the case in those early days.

Returning to the coal trade, further collieries had been sunk by John Nixon at Mountain Ash in 1853 (Navigation Colliery), and by David Davis at Abercwmboy (later spelt Abercwmboi) in 1856. The latter colliery was on the hillside across the mouth of the Aman valley from the Aberaman Ironworks and Colliery. Coal was won at Abercwmboy in 1859 and the Taff laid a short siding in towards the colliery from the up main line, this being extended by the colliery owner to the foot of the hillside where yet a further inclined plane led up to a colliery itself. On the other hand, Nixon had to sink very deep to reach coal at Navigation and it was not until 1860 that the colliery was finally opened. It was stated to be the deepest mine in the British Isles at the time.

One can only marvel at the faith of these pioneers of the coal industry who would spend seven years, at enormous expense, sinking into the bowels of the earth to reach the coveted black diamonds. Nixon, a practical engineer who invented several safety devices connected with mine working, was a Durham man born at Barlow, seven miles from Newcastle, in 1815, and had started work on his father's farm at the age of 14. He came to the Aberdare Valley in 1840 and, having for a short while previously been a mining engineer to an English company with collieries in France, he persuaded Thomas Powell that he could market Duffryn coal in that country.

Nixon did just that and had little difficulty in convincing the French market of the superior qualities of Aberdare coal. He then approached the French Minister of Marine, which led to the export of Aberdare coal for the French Navy. Following a dispute over commission rates with Powell, he sank his own pit at Werfa (already mentioned) in 1844 and struck the famous 'four foot' seam of coal. To strike coal at Navigation he had to sink deeper than anyone before, and through rock of colossal hardness and extent. For this venture he had Mr William Cory as a partner (another famous name in the South Wales coal industry) and the pit became the greatest and most important undertaking in Wales up to this time. The partners had previously purchased Deep Duffryn Colliery from David Williams.

Navigation was a much larger project, and when it opened on 12th May, 1860 there was a grand ceremony.

Flags and banners decorated the streets of Mountain Ash where a general holiday had been proclaimed. John Nixon performed the opening ceremony, his speech recalling the development of the coal trade in the valley from the beginning. He quoted figures to show the enormous increase in exports from Cardiff, where a second dock (the East Dock) had recently been opened, resulting in prosperity in that town besides the valley itself. He stated, amidst cheers, that there was no steam coal of better quality than that produced in the valley, and that tests carried out by the Admiralty, and elsewhere, had proved this beyond doubt.

In the summer of 1857, following the crossing complaints, the TVR had entered into an agreement with the Aberdare Local Board of Health to erect a footbridge at the side of the level crossing. By 8th October the bridge had not been started and Fisher reminded his Board that 'the erection of a footbridge for passengers at the Aberdare Level Crossing was urgently necessary', and that as the company had agreed to erect same 'the sooner done the better'. The bridge was completed early in 1858.

As early as 1855 a petition had gone to the TVR seeking the re-opening of Mill Street station. Fisher was not keen on the idea and told the Board that considerable alterations would have to be made before passenger trains could run on the section again. At the time passenger trains had run to Mill Street the mineral traffic was inconsiderable, but had increased beyond all expectation. With collieries so close to the line above the Aberdare Crossing, shunting movements took place on the main line, in addition to the running of the booked trains. If passenger trains were permitted, a separate line, and sidings at Mill Street should be provided. He added that there was still no proper public road to the Mill Street site. As usual the Board accepted Fisher's advice, and rejected the application.

It was in a report for the year 1850 that Fisher first mentioned 'Private Owner Wagons' although there is some evidence that they existed prior to that date on the TVR. By the end of 1850 Thomas Powell had 152 coal wagons on the Aberdare branch, also two of the older flat wagons for carrying boxes of coal; David Davis had 20 coal wagons, but Crawshay Bailey was only credited with 'five trucks'. Messrs Thomas and Joseph had three coal, and four coke wagons. These, and other proprietors, were hiring other wagons from the TVR.

With the growth of the coal trade the numbers of privately owned wagons greatly increased, and a list for 31st December, 1861 details the wagons owned, and hired, by the freight forwarders on the branch, and also gives the percentage of these wagons fitted with spring buffers and drawhooks.

Company	Number Wagons Owned	% Spring Buffers	Hired From TVR	% Spring Buffers
Aberdare Iron Co.	318	69	41	100
Aberdare Coal Co.	110	91	20	100
Amman Coal Co.	96	100	-	-
Crawshay Bailey	37	89	20	100
David Davis	67	72	288	100
Gadlys Iron Co.	131	99	25	92
Thomas & Joseph	65	100	41	100
Nixon, Taylor & Co.	461	99	-	-
Thos. Powell & Sons	439	70	485	82
Shepherd & Evans	51	98	103	98
Samuel Thomas	120	96	-	-
Lletty Shenkin Coal Co.	-	-	175	100

Thus a total of 3,093 wagons were in regular use in the Aberdare valley, not counting TVR wagons in normal goods train use. The percentage of wagons fitted with spring buffers and drawhooks at that early date is rather surprising. The numbers of hired wagons decreased sharply after 1857. Prior to that date the hiring charge was £10 per wagon per annum, but in 1857 the TVR gave notice that the charge was to be increased to £11 per annum. This resulted in most traders obtaining their own wagons in preference to hiring, and the Taff was left with hundreds of wagons on its hands, forcing a reduction in charges to £9 10s. 0d. per annum. Even so, with so many traders having obtained their own wagons, the Taff had difficulty in hiring them out.

The 1850s saw the start of a series of disputes between the Taff and the traders, also between the Taff and competing railways that were edging their way into the valley, which the Taff considered its own private preserve.

The Vale of Neath Railway (V of N) was the first to dispute the Taff's self-styled ownership of the transport rights in the valley. Entering the valley from the west, to a terminus at Aberdare, in 1851, it presented no serious threat, but when it branched out into the developing Dare and Aman valleys in the mid- and late-1850s the company became an active competitor. The Taff had previously thought the Aman valley traffic secure by Crawshay Bailey's private branch but this, beyond Aberaman, was nothing more than a horse drawn tramway and included an inclined plane, and was not in a position to compete effectively with the vale of Neath branch. When the V of N extended from Aberdare first to Canal Head in 1853, and finally to Middle Duffryn in 1856, they had access to most of the important collieries in the valley, and presented a real threat to the Taff.

The next main entrant was from the east, the GWR in 1864. Starting out as the Newport, Abergavenny and Hereford Railway's Taff Vale Extension, the Taff had quickly sized up the threat from this quarter and had formed an alliance with that company. The NA&H had originally intended to construct its own line from Quaker's Yard to Merthyr, but the Taff had persuaded the Newport company to connect with its line at Quaker's Yard, and use the TVR line to Merthyr. Similarly, in 1856-7, when the NA&H had dreams of extending from Quaker's Yard right through the Aberdare valley and thence on to Swansea, the Taff had again persuaded them that their best course was to connect with the TVR at Middle Duffryn and use the TVR line through to Aberdare and Mill Street, and continue their Swansea extension from that point. All the TVR asked in return for the running powers was that the NA&H should leave the Cardiff export coal trade to itself; the Taff would, in turn, leave the inland coal trade to the Newport company. All seemed very simple at the time, the NA&H had no Cardiff connections, and the Taff were not particularly interested in the inland trade.

Unfortunately for the Taff the new railway changed hands twice during construction of its extension, first to the West Midland Railway in 1860, and finally to the GWR in 1863, and the new companies were of different mind to the NA&H. When the main connection was made to Middle Duffryn in 1864 it was to the Vale of Neath line, and not the TVR, only a compensatory connection being made with the TVR at Mountain Ash the same year. With the GWR came the London and North Western railway, who used the GWR line to enter the valley.

Following Thomas Powell's death in 1863 the Powell Duffryn Steam Coal Company had been created. The latter, always being in dispute with the Taff over its high freight charges, had built its own railway between 1872-4 to connect its lower Aman valley collieries with the GWR line, thus further depriving the Taff of what had hitherto had been almost exclusively its own traffic. The worst blow of all came in 1871 when the Rhymney Railway gained a new access to the valley (its original one via Hengoed required reversals) by connecting with the NA&H Taff Vale Extension at Penallta Junction, and thence by running powers over the GWR to Middle Duffryn. Coal could then be taken to Cardiff from collieries on the Taff's doorstep, and shipped at the docks without passing over a yard of TVR metals. It was indeed fortunate that the Aberdare Valley coal trade continued to expand throughout the 1850s and from the modest 88,117 tons of mineral traffic the Taff had taken to Cardiff during 1847, this had risen to no less than 1,665,789 tons during 1863. The same year the coal output for the whole valley had been 2,538, 071 tons, so the Taff could hardly complain of the size of its share of the spoils at the time.

Despite the expansion there were periods of acute depression. In 1858-9 due to a temporary lack of markets, the miners were forced to accept a reduction in wages. The gloomy news was only relieved in the newspapers with a report of a freak shower of fish over Mountain Ash area on the morning of Wednesday 9th February, 1859. The report that it had been a very wet morning (nothing unusual in the valleys of South Wales) with a stiff south-west wind. Just as the up passenger train arrived at Mountain Ash - a little before 11 o'clock, the first shower of fish fell, spreading over the road and houses for a length of some 80 yards. The fish were said to have been alive and measuring from two to five inches long each. For good measure a second similar shower occurred 10 minutes later.

That depression, like the fish, soon cleared up, but for the next few years there was uneasiness both by the colliery owners and the miners due to each employer making terms with his own employees, causing differences between pits. Hence, on 14th March, 1864 the owners in the Aberdare valley combined to form the Aberdare Steam Collieries Association, its 14 members including the Powell Duffryn Company, John Nixon and David Davis. The associations' coalfields had produced some 1,600,000 tons in 1863, representing about 15 per cent of the output of the entire South Wales coalfield. Being confined to the Aberdare valley the association had its limitations, and in 1873 it was extended to include owners from other parts of South Wales, and the title altered to the Monmouthshire and South Wales Coalowners Association, its members controlling about 75 per cent of the output of the entire South Wales coalfield.

A financial collapse in 1866 had a serious effect on the demand for coal and, as far as the Aberdare coalfield was concerned was doubly serious as the adjacent Rhondda Valley coalfield was rapidly expanding at the time, in fact its output overtook that of the Aberdare coalfield a few years later. This meant a lot of the export trade passed to the Rhondda Valley, and coupled with the 1866 depression meant that most Aberdare miners had to accept a 5 per cent reduction in wages. This did not apply to the collieries connected with the ironworks, however; the masters decided that as their miners were not connected with the export trade they should be treated like the iron workers.

The depression was, to some extent, eased by the opening of the Dare Valley Railway by 1st July, 1866. This short tributary valley opened out to the town of Aberdare itself, and although barely two miles in length, contained some of the richest coal deposits in such a small area as could be found in South Wales. The Dare Valley Railway was leased to the TVR from the start and amalgamated with that company in 1889. It was difficult for train working; much of the line was on a gradient of 1 in 30.

An abortive scheme about this time, which may have remotely affected Aberdare valley rail traffic, was the proposed rail connection from the head of the TVR's Rhondda Fawr branch to the Hirwain area, in order to gain access to the collieries on Hirwain Common and also the traffic from Hirwain ironworks. A company called the Rhondda and Hirwain Junction Railway (RV&HJR) was promoted, with TVR backing, to construct a line from a junction with the TVR west of Treherbert (Blaenrhondda Junction) to connect with both the GWR (Vale of Neath section) and the private railways in the Hirwain area.

The RV&HJR secured its Act of Incorporation on 12th August, 1867 but with the trade recession over the next few years coupled with the reduced demand for iron products, it was just not worth the very heavy expenditure necessary to burrow a tunnel under the mountain range between the Rhondda and Hirwain areas. The first 1½ miles of the line from the TVR junction to Blaenrhondda Colliery was opened in 1878, but by its act of 17th June of the same year the company abandoned the remainder and obtained powers to lease the colliery branch to the TVR. As the railway thus never affected the Aberdare valley nothing more need be said of it here.

Whilst the depression partially eased in the later 1860s, it returned in the early 1870s and culminated in the closure of all four ironworks in the Aberdare area, along with some of the Powell Duffryn collieries, in 1875. The ironworks which closed, never to re-open, were at Llwydcoed, Abernant, Gadlys and Aberaman. The collieries closed were High Duffryn and Upper Duffryn (Cwmbach branch), Cwmneol (Aman Valley), Abergwawr (Aberdare) and Lower Duffryn (Cwmpennar). Of these Abergwawr and the two Cwmbach collieries never re-opened.

At the end of 1865 two new engine sheds were erected at Aberdare, to house 10-12 engines which had been formerly housed at Cardiff and worked up in the morning.

Chapter Five

Pulling Out of Depression

Until the depression in the mid-1860s the Aberdare Canal had managed to keep its head above water, despite the intense railway competition. Its trade in 1848, two years after the Aberdare Railway had opened, was 159,653 tons, which, despite the Aberdare Railway connecting to the north bank collieries to which it did not have access in 1848, coupled with the entry of the Vale of Neath Railway into the valley itself, actually increased to 216,704 tons in 1858. This was mainly due to the phenomenal increase in coal production in the 1850s, plus the fact that local shopkeepers and other small traders still used the canal as they refused to pay the high carriage rates demanded by the TVR.

The depression, however, coupled with the entry of the GWR into the valley from the east in 1864, caused traffic on the canal to decline, and the total for the year 1868 had dropped to 93,542 tons. Lord Bute took over the canal in 1885, but after checking the downward trend for a short period, traffic declined once again and the canal was finally closed in November 1900. In 1923 it was sold to the Aberdare and Mountain Ash Urban District Councils, and the land used to build the 'new road' that runs along the north side of the valley, itself supplanted in recent years by the Aberdare by-pass.

These depressions naturally affected the coal traffic taken down to the docks by the TVR. Despite the 1859 slump this trade had continued to increase until 1863, but declined to 1,422,300 tons in 1867. An improvement in the later 1860s resulted in 1,626,082 tons in 1869, but the decision of the Powell Duffryn Company to send some of their coal by the GWR route meant a drop to 1,213,996 tons carried by the TVR from the Aberdare Valley in 1871. Still worse was to come, as following the completion of the Powell Duffryn's own railway to the GWR in 1874 traffic declined alarmingly, and by 1878 only 616,345 tons passed down to Cardiff and Penarth by the TVR.

Brighter times were ahead however. A Paddington Agreement of 8th August, 1877, between the GWR, Taff and Rhymney Railways resulted in hostility between the competing railways being generally eliminated, and whilst the Rhymney continued to take a sizeable proportion of the Aberdare coal to Cardiff, there is no doubt that the Taff were the chief benefactors from the agreement. Furthermore another major colliery was opening out at the lower end of the valley directly accessible only to the TVR line. This was Penrhiwceiber (later spelled Penrikyber) Navigation Colliery, sunk by Messrs Glasbrook & Co., about 1½ miles south-east of Mountain Ash in 1873. The colliery was adjacent to the up side of the Aberdare branch.

At that time there were few houses in the Penrhiwceiber area, and when the colliery started producing coal in the early 1880s lack of transport for the miners to and from Mountain Ash caused petitions to be sent to the Taff to open a station near the new colliery. By that time housing had not developed in the Penrhiwceiber area sufficiently for the Taff to agree the request, but on 28th

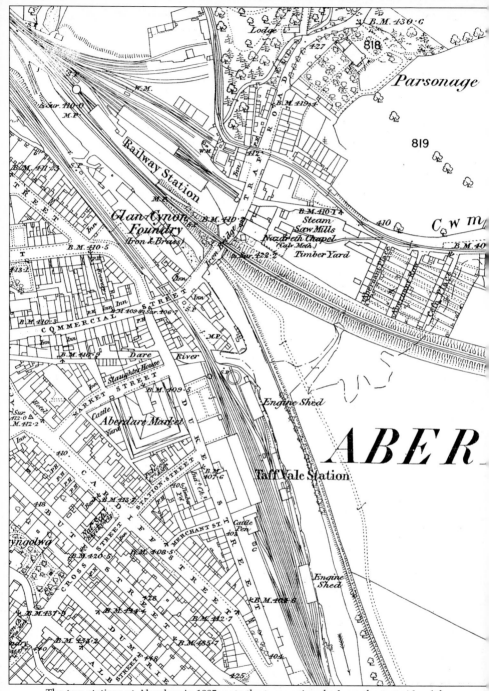

The two stations at Aberdare in 1885; note the two engine sheds on the east side of the TVR station. The line shown north of the GWR is the Hirwain tramroad from Canal Head.

Reproduced from the 25", 1885 Ordnance Survey Map

April, 1881, George Fisher was instructed to arrange for a workmen's train to run each morning and evening between Mountain Ash and the colliery, the colliery company to pay £30 a month for the service. This sufficed for the time being, but with housing rapidly springing up near the colliery, a request was made for the TVR Board to meet a deputation on the question of a passenger station.

The meeting was held on 27th April, 1882, the Directors still being very wary of putting up a proper station. They told the deputation that they were already receiving complaints that their passenger trains were stopping at too many small places, but they would visit the site and give their decision later. A month later the colliery company again wrote asking for the erection of a station but it was a further year before they had their wish granted.

Penrhiwceiber station opened on 1st June, 1883; initially certain trains only were stopped there, but the station must have been well patronised, as later in June the Taff announced that as from 1st July all branch passenger trains would stop here. A goods station was opened here in 1887. Apart form the railmotor 'Platforms', this was the last station to be erected on the branch. On 26th October, 1888 Treaman station was renamed Aberaman by authorisation of the Board, though its new name did not appear in timetables until next August. This must not be confused with the original Aberaman station, which had been nearer to Aberaman House, the residence of Crawshaw Bailey. A new station for Aberdare junction was authorised late in 1874. Fisher reported on 17th September, 1874 that 'there was no proper station at that place, simply a temporary timber structure without any of the ordinary conveniences for passengers'. He proposed a station building with a verandah all round, giving covered accommodation 150 ft long by 35 ft wide, at an estimated cost of £3,700. The station was completed the following year. Aberdare Junction station was renamed Abercynon as from 1st December, 1896, when further alterations were made.

The redoubtable George Fisher retired in August 1883, and was appointed 'Resident Director' and later Deputy Chairman. Despite the harsh words said about him in 1855 over the closure of Aberdare Junction station there is no doubt that he was the mainstay of the company in its early years. He started with the Taff in 1841, a few months after the line had been opened, and during his long career had occupied the posts of General Superintendent, Engineer, and later still, General Manager. On retirement the Board elected him a Director.

Although Aberdare Junction got a new station, the TVR stations at Cardiff and Aberdare were coming in for a lot of criticism in 1883. One correspondent in the *Cardiff Times*, on 19th May, 1883, referred to both stations as 'doghouses'. He continued 'at both places there is an utter want of decent conveniences; both erections were put up for mere temporary purposes more than 40 years ago [actually 37 years for Aberdare], and contained only the barest conveniences for the population of those days'. Aberdare's population had increased from about 7,000 to 38,000 during that period. Whilst, however, Cardiff got its new Queen Street station, completed in September 1887, Aberdare had to wait until 1914 before it had a new station.

Fisher himself had drawn the Directors' attention to the station 20 years before the letter in the *Cardiff Times*. He recommended the erection of a new station 'lower down the yard', but no action was taken.

A further effort to obtain a better station was made by the Aberdare Local Board of Health in 1890, who suggested the possibility of a new joint station with the GWR. After considerable correspondence between the two railway companies, the TVR Secretary replied that 'the very considerable expenditure involved would not be justified by the number of passengers to whom a joint station would be of any convenience'.

Another regular bone of contention was the road level crossing at Commercial Street, Aberdare. As early as 27th December, 1856, there had been complaints about it. It had been stated that the roadway was frequently blocked for up to 20 minutes whilst engines were making up their trains. Foot passengers, horsemen, and vehicles were completely jammed up, waiting for the gates to open. Although the problem was partially alleviated by the erection in 1858 of the footbridge already referred to, obviously the position was worsened for road traffic with the opening of the Dare Valley Railway in 1866.

By 1885 the Aberdare Local Board of Health were still complaining of the delays caused by the crossing, and after several months of correspondence with the Taff, the railway company, in December 1885, made the classic comment that they would in future, during the hours of darkness, light a lamp on top of the footbridge. The Chairman of the Local Board made the caustic comment 'this is a wonderful concession on the part of the company. Of course it does away with the nuisance in one broad sweep'. He asked the surveyor to make a report on the number of times the gates were closed, also the estimated cost of making a subway in lieu of the footbridge. The Surveyor kept a check on trains on Saturday 16th, January, 1886, and the following Monday, Tuesday and Wednesday, for 12 hours each day commencing at 7.30 am. His report showed that the gates had been closed 25, 23, 21 and 30 times respectively, the total daily delays being 44, 41, 40 and 55 minutes. With an average delay of less than two minutes, and an estimated cost of £1,200 for the proposed subway, the matter was allowed to stand over.

Such matters were, however, of minor importance compared with the opposition the Taff had from the various railway companies endeavouring to get a foothold in the Aberdare valley. The companies that succeeded have already been mentioned, but mention should be made here of those that fell by the wayside, mainly due to TVR opposition. These railways were promoted in the early 1860s, the first two with somewhat similar aims. The Aberdare Northern Railway Company was promoted with LNWR support to construct a railway from the Aberdare railway at Mill Street, to connect with the Neath and Brecon Railway at Devynock and thence, by running powers and connections, to the north of the country via Craven Arms and Shrewsbury. This railway would have sought running powers over the whole length of the Aberdare Railway. The Aberdare and Central Wales Junction Railway was promoted with much the same object in view. It would have made a junction with the

Aberdare Railway just west of Aberdare station, and continued its own line to a junction with the Central Wales railway, from where running powers would be obtained to north-west England.

The third proposed railway was the Aberdare Valley and Caerphilly Junction Railway; this was the brainchild of George Elliott, who was now in charge of the Powell Duffryn empire. This company would have connected with the GWR near Mountain Ash at one end of the line, and to the Rhymney Railway east of Caerphilly at the other end. Its aim was to divert Aberdare valley coal traffic to Newport Docks via the Rhymney and Brecon and Merthyr Railways. A similar aim was the basis of the later Pontypridd, Caerphilly and Newport Railway (PC&N), which opened in 1884. Construction of the latter railway was the reason why Nixons Navigation Company built their private railway through the lower half of the Aberdare Valley. The PC&N Act, 8th August, 1878, authorised a line from the Rhymney Railway at Penrhos Junction (Caerphilly) to the Taff Vale Railway at PC&N Junction, immediately south of Pontypridd station. This would enable coal from the colliery areas on the TVR system to pass directly to Newport Docks via the PC&N line, and thence by running powers over the Rhymney, Brecon and Merthyr and Great Western railways to Newport Docks.

Despite gaining this Act the PC&NR were ambitious to obtain Aberdare Valley coal without this traffic passing over the TVR system at all. In 1883 they put in a further Bill to Parliament seeking authority to extend their line up the east side of the Taff valley, from just north of Glyntaff as far as the old canal basin at Aberdare Junction (Railway No. 1). At the same time agreement was reached with Messrs Nixon and Powell Duffryn, both of whom were always seeking a cheaper route to the docks for their export coal traffic, whereby Nixon agreed to build his own railway from Navigation Colliery to a point near the canal basin, where a head-on junction would be made with the proposed PC&N extension. From the west end of Nixon's line the PC&N would lay a further extension (Railway No. 2) to the terminus of the Powell Duffryn Railway at Middle Duffryn. In this way coal from the Aman Valley collieries, also from Middle Duffryn, Deep Duffryn and Navigation collieries, could be sent to Newport Docks without passing over any part of the TVR, and only over short sections of the Rhymney Railway (in the Caerphilly area) and the GWR (from Bassaleg Jn to Newport) both by means of running powers.

Provision was made for the PC&N to work the line throughout as far as Middle Duffryn, with Nixon responsible for his own sidings (adjacent to the proposed line) in the Mountain Ash area, and Powell Duffryn to work its own line from Middle Duffryn into the Aman Valley. Due to the TVR and other opposition Parliament refused to authorise the PC&N extension, thus early in 1884 Nixon was left with a partially finished line running south-eastwards from Navigation Colliery towards Aberdare Junction, this line being on the north bank of the River Cynon, between the Taff Vale and Great Western lines through the valley. Nixon had little alternative but to make an agreement with the TVR, signed on 31st March, 1884, for him to complete his private line by a junction with the TVR at Pontcynon, just under one mile inside the valley from

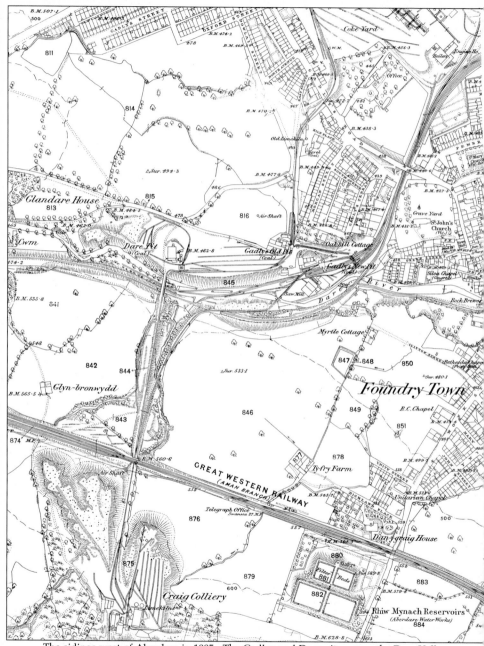

The sidings west of Aberdare in 1885. The Gadlys and Dare pits are on the Dare Valley branch, half a mile from its junction north of Aberdare station. Note the tramway from Craig Colliery climbing over the branch and Dare river to overhead tips at Gadlys New Pit, and also over the branch to Dare Pit, Old Pit, and the coke yard. The siding (*top right*) led to the Ironworks (later a wagon works).

Reproduced from the 25", 1885 Ordnance Survey Map

Aberdare Junction. Hence Nixon's railway, from Navigation Colliery to the TVR at Pontcynon Junction was opened for traffic, without ceremony, during the week-ending Saturday 15th November, 1884.

Shortly afterwards the line proved a greater asset to Nixon than he expected in 1884. In the mid-1880s he started sinking a major colliery at Cwmcynon, a short distance west of Penrhiwceiber. This colliery, which started production in 1890, was adjacent to the private railway, and its traffic could conveniently be sent direct to the docks via Pontcynon Junction, without in any way interfering with the traffic from Navigation Colliery. So, with two major collieries adjacent to his private railway Nixon had two outlets/inlets to the TVR, the original one from Navigation Colliery sidings at Nixon's Lower Junction, immediately west of Mountain Ash station, and at Pontcynon Junction at the lower end of the valley.

Nixon's railway was single track for most of its length.   On leaving Pontcynon Junction it immediately crossed over the River Cynon where, on the north bank, storage and reception sidings were laid out. From these sidings the branch continued single line to Cwmcynon Colliery sidings, with a single line by-pass around these sidings to continue direct to the sidings at Navigation Colliery.   The extent of the private railway was almost three miles, and connections were also made to the GWR line, both for Cwmcynon Colliery and at Mountain Ash. West of Mountain Ash Nixon's sidings continued the short distance to Deep Duffryn Colliery, this section having been laid in 1861.

Late in 1889 the TVR laid a third line of rails between Pontcynon Junction and Cynon Crossing (Abercynon North). When opened, early in 1890, this was used as a single line for all passenger trains, the two existing lines being used as up and down mineral roads. The single line passenger section was worked by Electric Train Staff, and remained a passenger single line section until the withdrawal of passenger services in 1964.

The sidings put in for Penrhiwceiber Colliery were of particular interest as they were initially laid on the formation for the severe curve around the bend in the river which had caused so much trouble in the 1850s. The colliery was adjacent to the south side of the curve, and whilst sinking was in progress a siding was laid to it over the west half of the curve. Following opening of the colliery in 1881 a second siding over the original formation of the east half of the curve was put in, the two sidings, in effect, forming the same path as the original Aberdare Railway had done. Even the colliery company found the complete curve too severe and later eased the west side, although the eastern siding into the colliery was still on the original 1846 Aberdare Railway bed. The two connections with the Taff Vale line were known as Penrhiwceiber Upper and Lower Junctions.

A further colliery, Glyn Gwyn Level, was opened by Nixon's in 1889. This 'house coal' colliery was close to Navigation, but on the hillside south of the TVR line, and only served directly by a tramroad. In more recent times a further colliery was opened called Abergorki; this was immediately east of Navigation Colliery, in fact it could easily be mistaken for an extension of the latter colliery. Glyn Gwyn closed in the mid-1920s, about the same time as Abergorki started production. The latter, which was served direct by Nixon's railway, closed in 1967.

Two further small pits were also opened in the same area. The first, at which coal was struck in 1885, was called Miskin Colliery. This was sited east of Glyn Gwyn Level and almost adjacent to the TVR line. It was mainly a 'house coal' colliery, and lasted until 1914. The other, called Pentwyn Merthyr, was east of Penrikyber Navigation Colliery. This was opened by D.R. Jones in 1916, but had a very short life, being closed about 10 years later.

In the early years of the present century a short loop was put in to the south of the TVR line between Pontcynon Junction and Penrikyber Colliery. This served a short tramway leading to Ynysboeth Quarry. For some strange reason the Taff official names for the junctions with the main line at each end of the loop were called Ynysboeth *Colliery* Upper and Lower Junctions. The loop was taken out during World War I.

The later standard class of 0-6-0 was the 'L' class; here one is shunting Nixons Navigation empties at Mountain Ash about 1900.

Chapter Six

Invasion From All Sides

In the late 1880s a further shipping outlet for Aberdare Valley and other South Wales coal was under construction, much to the anger of the TVR, which initially lost considerable revenue as a result. This was Barry Dock, which opened in July 1889. Coal traffic from the Aberdare Valley, destined for shipment at this dock, was handed over to the Barry Railway at Treforest Junction, from which it took that company's direct route to the new dock. Hence by 1889 Aberdare coal was being shipped at no less than five South Wales ports, from east to west, Newport, Cardiff, Penarth, Barry and Swansea, with still a little at Briton Ferry thrown in for good measure.

Two further abortive schemes which would have given direct rail access to the Aberdare coalfield failed in the mid-1890s. The first was embodied in a Bill which the Bute Docks Company (from 1897 renamed the Cardiff Railway Company) put to Parliament in the winter session of 1895/6. This sought powers for the Docks Company to acquire undertakings of the Glamorganshire and the Aberdare Canal Navigations, and to convert large sections of the canals into railways. The scheme was to build a railway over the Glamorgan canal from Cardiff to the junction with the Aberdare canal at Navigation (Abercynon), and continue with the railway over the path of the Aberdare canal to Canal Head. The main purpose was to provide a direct alternative to the TVR for Aberdare valley coal destined for shipment at Cardiff Docks. It was, however, the intention to make it a passenger line with stations at Aberdare (facing Cwmbach Road), and also at Treforest, Nantgarw and Cardiff.

A public meeting was convened by the High Constable, and held at the Court Room, New Public Hall, Aberdare on Wednesday 29th January, 1896, for the purpose of supporting the objects of the Bill. The usual complaints about the TVR's high freight charges were brought up, and one trader stated that when he had complained to the TVR about slow delivery of his goods he had been told 'Don't send your goods with us, we have got quite enough trade in coal'. The meeting unanimously passed a resolution supporting the objects of the Bill but, nevertheless, the TVR opposition in Parliament was successful in getting it rejected. The Bute Docks Company, like the PC&N a few years earlier, had to be content with its 1897 Act which authorised a railway from Cardiff to connect with the TVR line south of Pontypridd, in this case at Treforest, a junction which the Taff prevented ever being brought into use commercially.

The second ambitious railway company was the North Pembroke and Fishguard, which also cast envious eyes on the coal traffic flowing from the valley. Despite their limited resources this company, in their Bill for the 1896/7 session of Parliament, sought powers to construct a railway connecting with the TVR in the Gadlys area, just west of the road level crossing at Aberdare, with running powers over the Taff line throughout the Aberdare coalfield. This section of the Bill was hotly opposed, not only by the TVR but also by the

An early photograph of Aberdare TVR station before it was rebuilt in red brick.

C. Chapman Collection

Light engines wait at Aberdare; the main engine shed is behind. The leading engine is an 'L' class 0-6-0 and the the other an '01' class 0-6-2T.

Oakwood Collection

Aberdare UDC (which had replaced the old Board of Health as from 1st January, 1895). The latter viewed with concern any further train movements over the level crossing. The combined opposition resulted in the relevant section of the Bill being thrown out.

By the mid-1890s the Aberdare branch was virtually complete, although there were some major alterations at Cwmbach Junction in 1900. To all intents and purposes part of the Taff Vale system, it still remained only leased to that company by the Aberdare Railway. The fortunate shareholders of the latter company were still receiving their 10 per cent per annum in good times and bad. In 1901, however, the Taff Board decided the time had come for the Aberdare Company to be vested in its undertaking. This was achieved by the Taff Vale Railway Act dated 31st July, 1902, the actual amalgamation of the companies taking place as from 30th June, 1902. The Aberdare shareholders received £164 of TVR 3 per cent Debenture Stock for each £50 share in the capital of the Aberdare Railway, thus maintaining their 10 per cent dividend.

The only later additions on the branch were the steam railcar Platforms erected in the early years of the present century, these being the result of threatened road competition. The first such competition had come as early as 1873 when a horse bus had started running between Cap Coch (now Abercwmboi) and Aberdare. This was run by a company called the Aberdare and Aberaman Omnibus Company, which commenced a service between the two places on 1st September, 1873, with five return trips each day and one extra late journey on Saturday evenings. The service, which was later extended to Aberdare Mill Street, was greatly appreciated by the residents, who still had a train service of only four each way on weekdays, and two only on Sundays. Further, the horse bus served the housing much better than the train. particularly in the Aberaman-Abercwmboi area.

This service was superseded by an early motor bus service run by the Aberdare Valley Motor Car Company, which secured a licence from the UDC to operate the same in November 1899. Services were run between Aberdare and Aberaman, also between Aberdare and Trecynon, although the latter proved unprofitable and was withdrawn. Even the main service did not last long, being terminated on 31st December, 1904 but did serve, with various schemes brought forward at the time to run electric street tramcar services in the area, to draw the TVR's attention to the need for an improvement in the local rail service.

In all fairness, there had been a big improvement in the passenger train service in the last decade of the 19th century. Following the introduction of the more versatile tank engines for passenger work, a timetable of nine trains in each direction was being worked on the branch when the first signs of tramcar competition started in August 1899. On 26th August the Taff Board heard a report that an application had been made to the Light Railway Commissioners, by the British Electric Traction Company, for powers to construct a tramway 3¾ miles long, basically covering the route of the horse bus. The Board decided to oppose the application strongly and an enquiry was held at the Council Chamber at Aberdare on 10th January, 1900. The application was refused, but

Railcar No. 11, built by Kerr, Stuart & Co. in 1905; these one-class cars handled the workmen's trip from Mill Street up the Dare Valley. *LPC*

The Taff Vale Railway station at Mountain Ash, looking towards Aberdare.
B.J. Miller Collection

mainly on the technicality that the Light Railway Commissioners had no jurisdiction in the matter as the proposed light railway (tramway) was solely within the boundary of one local authority, i.e. the Aberdare Urban District Council.

Less than two years later application was made to the Board of Trade, by the Aberdare and Mountain Ash Urban District Councils, for Provisional Orders to construct street tramways in their areas. Once again the TVR provided strong opposition; again a local inquiry was held, on 11th March, 1902, and the following month it was announced that the Board of Trade had rejected the Tramway Schemes of the two councils.

In December 1903, in the face of street tramcar competition in many parts of its system, the TVR completed a steam rail car at its Cardiff Works, and gave it trials on both the main line and various branches. Its first trial on the Aberdare branch was on Wednesday 12th December, 1903. No. 1 Car settled down to regular service on the Cardiff-Penarth-Cadoxton section, and its success led to six further cars being ordered early in 1904, with a further six later that year. Whilst preparations were being made to start a service on the Aberdare branch, to commence in December 1904, an interim service was started in the local Aberdare area on Saturday 26th November.

Motor Platforms, as the Taff called them, were opened at Mill Street, roughly on the site of the station closed in 1852, and at Commercial Street, immediately west of the level crossing gates. Both Platforms had been authorised by the Board, Mill Street at an estimated cost of £106 on 31st May, 1904, and Commercial Street at a cost of £116 on 18th October. Also authorised on 31st May were further Platforms at Duffryn Crossing (£193) and at Pontcynon (£95). There would have to be two platforms at Duffryn to cover the up and down lines, but as there was only single line beyond Aberdare station, one platform sufficed at Mill Street and Commercial Street. At Pontcynon the platform was east of Nixon's Junction, and as the passenger traffic was worked on a single line from there to Abercynon North, again one platform sufficed.

The interim service between Mill Street and Aberdare station, only ¾ mile apart, started with one railcar on Saturday 26th November, as stated, the railcar not working to a timetable, but scheduled to run as often as required between 8 am and 6 pm. The railcar called at Commercial Street on each trip, the fare being 1d. standard whether going the whole way or to Commercial Street only. On the first day the demand kept the service running till 10 pm, by which time 1,094 passengers had been carried. (The Platforms at Aberdare and Commercial Street were closer together than any the author has known, their centres being only 220 yds apart.)

On 26th December, 1904 the planned railmotor service over the entire branch commenced. It was introduced as ' supplementing the ordinary train service'. The new service which operated between Mill Street and Pontypridd, stopped at all the stations and Platforms, whilst the ordinary train service, which still operated between Aberdare and Abercynon stations only (with some through carriages to Cardiff or Penarth) stopped only at the stations. The ordinary train service at the time was 12 each way, pus 1 workmen's train each

The Aberdare area. Note the Abernant Railway, which ran along the canal towpath to an end-on junction with the TVR's Cwmbach branch.

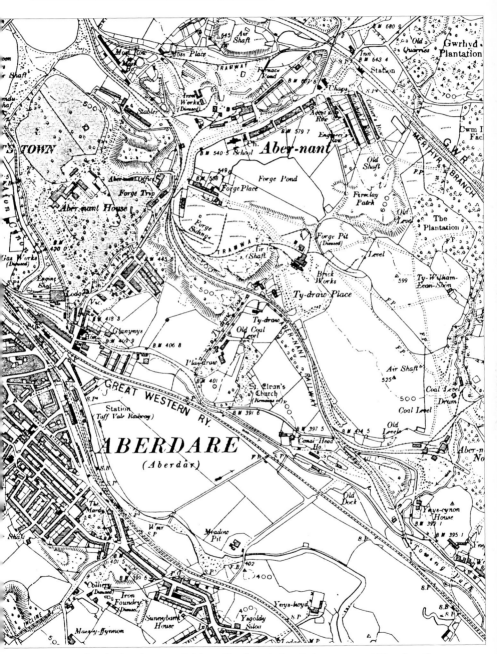

Note also that the line does not finish at Aberdare station, but runs on past Dare Junction and Gadlys Junction to the site of the original Mill Street station.

Reproduced from the 25", 1900 Ordnance Survey Map

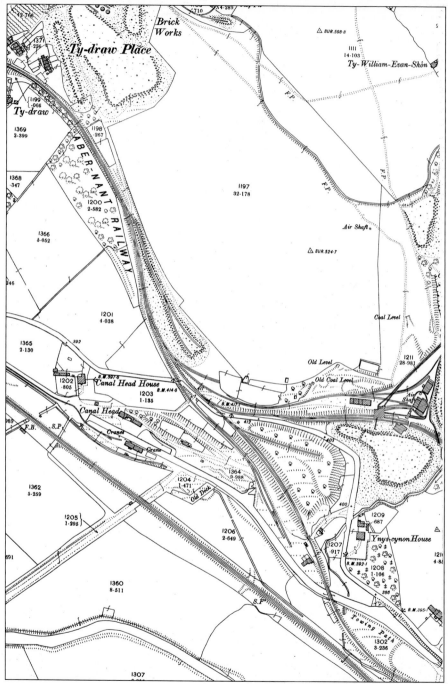

Lines east of Aberdare. The Abernant Railway replaced the tramroad from the Abernant ironworks and colliery to the canal; it was standard gauge and joined end-on to the TVR Cwmbach branch, which crossed the GWR on the level beyond Ynyscynon. Note that the tramroad from the canal head to Hirwain is still in place, though probably not in use.

Reproduced from the 25", 1900 Ordnance Survey Map

way. The supplementary railmotor service added a further six trips each way on the branch, plus two additional trips each way from Mill Street to Mountain Ash only. The populace must have considered themselves most fortunate to have some 20 services each way daily, also 4 extra Platforms, whereas only 20 years previously they had but 6 trains daily to choose from. Apart from the full branch service, the cars continued to fill in gaps in the timetable with short trips between Aberdare station, Commercial Street and Mill Street, 10 such trips on weekdays, with 5 extra on Saturday evenings. The railmotor service did not run on Sundays, there being four trains only each way that day.

Duffryn Crossing Platform was renamed Abercwmboi Platform as from 1st January, 1906. This motor station had staggered platforms, the up Platform being to the west of the footpath crossing, and the down Platform to the east. Mill Street and Commercial Street Platforms were closed in 1st June, 1912, although Mill Street continued in use for Dare Valley workmen's trains until the end of 1924, after the GWR had taken over control. Commercial Street was closed entirely. One further railmotor Platform was opened at Mathewstown, between Pontcynon Junction and Penrhiwceiber on 1st October, 1914, to cater for the growing population to the east of Penrhiwceiber, particularly in the Tynetown area.

With the Aberdare branch traffic at its height in the early years of the century it will be, it is hoped, interesting to give the official mileages of the various colliery branches, stations, motor Platforms etc., for the 8¼ miles from the branch junction at the south of Abercynon station, to Mill Street terminus. For added interest the list indicates whether the colliery or siding was on the up side (U) or down side (D), and whether it was facing (F) or trailing (T) junction, always looking in the Aberdare direction.

Official Mileages - Aberdare Branch

Location	Jn	From Cardiff Docks	
		M	C
Aberdare Branch Jn (Mineral)	UF	16	20
Abercynon Station	-	16	28
Abercynon North Jn (Pass.)	UF	16	33
Pontcynon Bridge Platform	-	17	16
Pontcynon Jn (Nixons)	DF	17	20
Ynysyboeth Colliery Lower Jn*	UF	17	50
Ynysyboeth Colliery Upper Jn*	UT	17	63
Penrhiwceiber Colliery Lower Jn	UF	18	14
Penrhiwceiber Colliery Upper Jn	UT	18	68
Penrhiwceiber Station	-	18	74
Mountain Ash Station	-	20	11
Nixon's Lower Jn (Navigation)	DT	20	17
GWR Jn	DT	20	18
Nixon's Upper Jn (Deep Duffryn)	DF	20	18
Lower Duffryn Jn (P.D. Co.)	DF	20	19
Duffryn Crossing Platform	-	21	9
Abercwmboi Colliery Lower Jn	UF	21	17
Middle Duffryn Colliery Jn	DF	21	24
Park Siding Jn (P.D. Ry.)	UT	21	76

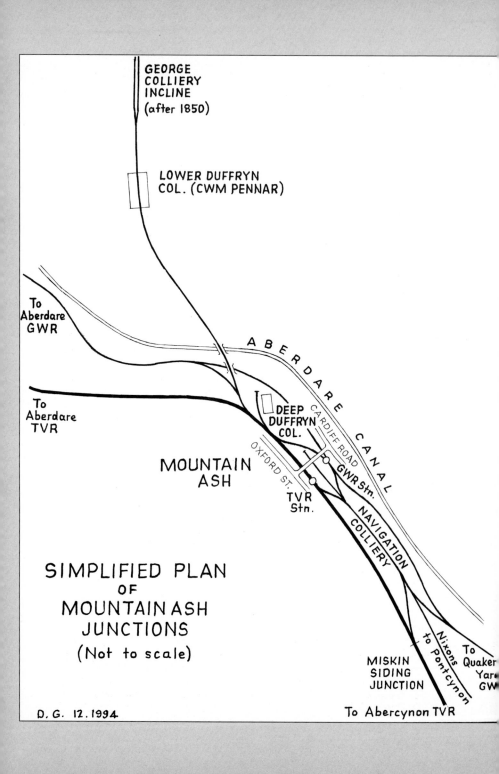

GEORGE
COLLIERY
INCLINE
(after 1850)

LOWER DUFFRYN
COL. (CWM PENNAR)

To
Aberdare
GWR

To
Aberdare
TVR

A B E R D A R E   C A N A L

DEEP
DUFFRYN
COL.

CARDIFF ROAD

MOUNTAIN
ASH

OXFORD ST.

GWR Stn.

NAVIGATION
COLLIERY

TVR
Stn.

SIMPLIFIED PLAN
OF
MOUNTAIN ASH
JUNCTIONS
(Not to scale)

Nixons
to Pontcynon

To
Quaker
Yard
GW

MISKIN
SIDING
JUNCTION

To Abercynon TVR

D.G. 12.1994

		From Cardiff Docks	
Location	Jn	M	C
Cwmbach Branch Jn	DF	22	1
(Lletty Shenkin Colliery Jn)	(DF)	(22	2)
(End of Cwmbach Branch)	-	(22	52
Tremain Colliery Jn (P.D. Ry.)	UT	22	52
Aberaman Station	-	22	54
Plough Pit Jn	UF	22	55
Abergwawr Upper Siding	UF	22	73
Aberdare Station	-	23	55
Commercial Street Platform	-	23	65
Dare Valley Jn	UF	23	73
(End of Dare Valley Branch)	-	(26	20)
Gadlys Jn (with GWR)	DF	23	76
(End on Jn with GWR)	-	(24	12)
Mill Street Platform	-	24	39
Mill Street Tinworks	-	24	39
End of Branch	_	24	41

* *Official names of junctions; actually served Ynysboeth Quarry*

The later Mathewstown Platform was sited at 18 miles 9 chains.

Commencement of the steam rail car services brought an immediate increase in passenger traffic, and an official report in May 1905 stated that an increase of 32 per cent had been achieved on the Aberdare branch. Even so, the demand for street tramcars, which were so popular throughout the land at the time, remained active despite the earlier setbacks. In November 1904 the Aberdare Council again published Parliamentary Notice that they were submitting a Bill in the ensuing Session for powers to construct tramways. Once again the Taff opposed vigorously and the Bill was rejected by the House of Commons Committee on 18th April, 1905. In November 1906 it was reported that a syndicate had been formed to promote a tramway from Aberdare to Cilfynydd (north of Pontypridd), to form a junction there with the Pontypridd Tramways. They obtained the blessing of Aberdare Urban District Council for the scheme, but the Mountain Ash Council refused their assent.

The next effort was a further Bill presented by the Aberdare Council in November 1910 which, despite the usual opposition from the Taff Vale Railway, passed the House of Lords Committee on 18th May, 1911, and the Commons Committee on 27th July. Trams started running the 2¾ miles between Trecynon and Aberaman on 9th October, 1913, the service being supplemented by four trolley bus feeder services. At the time the latter were called railless or trackless trolley routes, and operated between: Aberaman and Abercwmboi, Aberaman and Cwmaman, Aberdare and Abernant, and Trecynon and Cwmdare.

The first was purely an extension of the tramway route to the Abercwmboi area, whilst the other three were sideways feeders. Both tramway and trolley bus services were run by the Aberdare UDC Tramways and were reported at the time as being the first installation of the combined systems to operate in the country. The tram and bus depot was at Gadlys where a power station was installed.

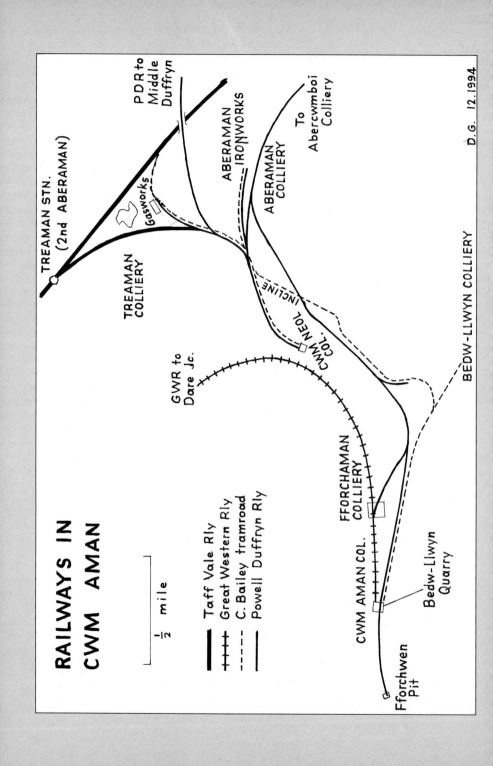

RAILWAYS IN CWM AMAN

$\frac{1}{2}$ mile

— Taff Vale Rly
+++ Great Western Rly
--- C. Bailey tramroad
— Powell Duffryn Rly

TREAMAN STN.
(2nd ABERAMAN)

PDR to Middle Duffryn

Gasworks

TREAMAN COLLIERY

ABERAMAN IRONWORKS

ABERAMAN COLLIERY

To Abercwmboi Colliery

GWR to Dare Jc.

CWM NEOL COL.

INCLINE

BEDW-LLWYN COLLIERY

FFORCHAMAN COLLIERY

CWM AMAN COL.

Bedw-Llwyn Quarry

Fforchwen Pit

D.G. 12.1994

The tramway system was extended in 1921/2 but the advent of petrol buses in the 1920s was the beginning of the end for the trams, which were finally abandoned in 1935 after a comparatively short life of less than 22 years. Buses have remained supreme since, with both Western Welsh and the Red and White companies once having garages at Aberdare, although the Western Welsh closed its depot in 1971.

Meanwhile further developments had taken place adjacent to the Taff line in the early years of the century. In 1903 the Powell Duffryn Company opened a central washery for small coal at Middle Duffryn, capable of washing 160 tons per hour. This catered for small coal washing for all the Powell Duffryn collieries in the Aberdare and Aman valley areas. An electric power station was opened at the same site about the same time, this also serving all the company's Aberdare collieries. The colliery at Middle Duffryn, together with Thomas Powell's original Duffryn colliery (Old Duffryn) had not raised coal since 1885, but from 1888 onwards both pits were used for pumping and/or ventilating shafts in connection with Tremain and Aberaman Collieries. When Tremain was abandoned in January 1911 both Middle and Old Duffryn pits were abandoned at the same time. The Middle Duffryn site, however, remained extremely busy from the railway point of view, being the central point for all Powell Duffryn traffic, both for despatch and for the washery and fuel works there. The latter had been erected in the late 1870s.

Other collieries officially abandoned in the early years of the century were Gadlys in 1902, Werfa in 1910, Lletty Shenkin in 1913 and Abercwmboi in 1914. All the former Aberdare Iron Company's collieries closed about the same time, River Level in 1897, Tunnel in 1904, the new Cwmbach Pit in 1908, No. 9 Pit in 1909 and Blaenant in 1913. Both Abercwmboi and Lletty Shenkin were retained by Powell Duffryn Company for a number of years, Lletty Shenkin until 1923; Abercwmboi, which had rarely been a profitable pit on its own account, was useful for pumping and ventilating, and was retained to prolong the useful life of Aberaman Colliery until comparatively recent times. It was still linked to Aberaman in the official *List of Mines* as late as 1948. The Powell Duffryn Company also acquired and re-opened two of the former iron company's pits, Blaenant in 1915 and River Level about 1917.

A new level was also started at the Werfa site about 1914 by the Werfa Dare Colliery Company. Production started two years later and this level, called Werfa Dare, survived until NCB days, being closed in August 1949. It was remarkable that it survived so long as a small private company as by 1938 all other collieries in the valley, apart from Penrikyber, had been embraced in the Powell Duffryn empire, and even that colliery was associated with Powell Duffryn from late 1942 onwards.

Retracing our steps to the colliery closures, by 1913 all rail traffic on the Cwmbach and Lletty Shenkin branches had ceased, but the Cwmbach branch was retained as, from its terminus, it continued by a head-on junction to the Abernant site by the former Abernant Ironworks railway. Within the area of the ironworks the iron company had opened River Level colliery in 1866. Although this colliery had been abandoned by the ironworks company's successors, the

Penrhiwceiber station looking towards Aberdare about 1920; the main building is on the left, and a goods train is just leaving, the signal being placed on the opposite side of the track.
Lens of Sutton

Aberaman station about 1920, looking up-valley; the points at bottom left were for the Treaman Siding, leading to the Aman Valley branch. *Lens of Sutton*

Aberdare Works and Collieries Company, in 1897, it was being re-developed by the Powell Duffryn Company, hence the Cwmbach branch and private railway (by then P.D. owned) were retained.

River Level restarted production in 1917 and its coal was routed via the private line to the TVR for despatch until the early 1930s. Then, as an economy measure, the GWR who by that time controlled the former TVR, closed the Cwmbach branch as a through route at the end of 1935 by taking out the rail level crossing over the Neath-Pontypool Road main line. After that date all coal from River Level Colliery was routed on to that main line via Cwmbach siding.

The Lletty Shenkin branch, which left the Cwmbach Junction, was closed in 1913, and the rails taken up; the bridge over the River Cynon was demolished.

On the railway itself the single line section between Aberdare North (immediately east of the crossing gates) and Dare Valley Junction was doubled in 1902, the up line becoming the passenger line when steam rail car services to Commercial Street and Mill Street Platforms started two years later. The down line was used for through coal traffic.

The Aberdare valley with its smoke, grime and pitheads was an area seldom selected for a Royal tour, but at least one Royal Train penetrated the lower end of the valley, even if most of the local part of the tour was undertaken by car. The date was Thursday 27th June, 1912, and Their Majesties King George V and Queen Mary were concluding a three day visit to Cardiff and selected places in the valleys of east South Wales. On that particular day when, in typical South Wales fashion, it rained throughout, Pontypridd, the Rhondda Valley and Dowlais were visited by the TVR Royal Train, the tour continuing through Merthyr and the Aberdare valley by motor car.

On entering Aberdare from Hirwain the Royal car passed under a massive triumphal arch, sited at the junction of Hirwain Road and Cwmdare Road, Trecynon, constructed entirely of huge blocks of coal. The structure comprised one main central arch, 16 feet in width, flanked by two smaller arches, each 7 ft wide, on either side. The side arches represented colliery underground roadways, each complete with a loaded tram of coal. The towers over each side were decorated with shields made up from miners picks and shovels, whilst over the centre arch were banners welcoming the Royal couple, and from the arch itself were suspended decorations consisting of Davy Miners' lamps. The whole structure, which was 50 ft in width, and almost 30 ft high up to the top of the side towers, was erected by the Bwllfa and Merthyr Dare Colliery Company under the guidance of Mr Rees Llewllyn, the Managing Director of the company. It was stated that the King was greatly impressed by this unusual from of welcome to Aberdare.

After visiting and appreciating Aberdare public park, which also pleased Their Majesties, and which the King later stated was one of extreme beauty and spaciousness for an industrial area, the tour then proceeded to Mountain Ash. Here a loyal address was presented, and thence the tour continued to Penrhiwceiber TVR station from where the Royal Train conveyed Their Majesties back to Cardiff. The train was stabled in readiness at the up platform to avoid the party having to cross the footbridge, and was due to depart at 5.40

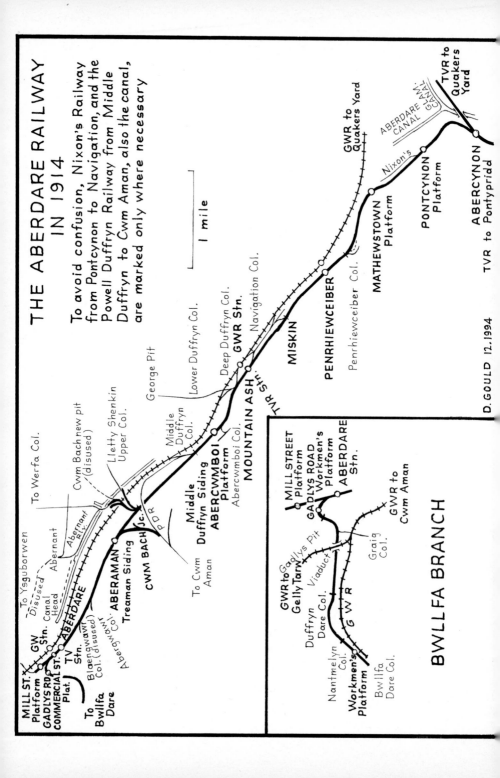

THE ABERDARE RAILWAY IN 1914

To avoid confusion, Nixon's Railway from Pontcynon to Navigation, and the Powell Duffryn Railway from Middle Duffryn to Cwm Aman, also the canal, are marked only where necessary

1 mile

D. GOULD 12.1994

TVR to Quakers Yard

GWR to Quakers Yard

ABERCYNON

TVR to Pontypridd

Aberdare Canal

GLAM. CANAL

Nixon's

PONTCYNON Platform

MATHEWSTOWN Platform

Penrhiewceiber Col.

PENRHIEWCEIBER

MISKIN

Navigation Col.

Deep Duffryn Col.

GWR Stn.

Lower Duffryn Col.

George Pit

TVR Stn.

MOUNTAIN ASH

Abercwmboi Col.

ABERCWMBOI Platform

Middle Duffryn Siding

To Cwm Aman

P.D.R.

CWM BACH Jc.

Middle Duffryn Col.

Lletty Shenkin Upper Col.

Cwm Bach new pit (disused)

To Werfa Col.

Abergwawr Rd.

Abernant

Canal Head

Abernant

To Ysguborwen

Disused

GW Stn.

MILL ST. Platform

GADLYS RD. Platform

COMMERCIAL ST. Plat.

TV Stn.

ABERDARE

Blaengwawr Col. (disused)

Abergwawr Col.

ABERAMAN

Treaman Siding

To Bwllfa Dare

BWLLFA BRANCH

MILL STREET Platform

GADLYS ROAD Workmen's Platform

ABERDARE Stn.

GWR to Gadlys
Gelly Tarw
Gelly Tarw/lys Pit

Duffryn Dare Col.

Viaduct

G W R

GWR to Cwm Aman

Graig Col.

Nantmelyn Col.

Workmen's Platform

Bwllfa Dare Col.

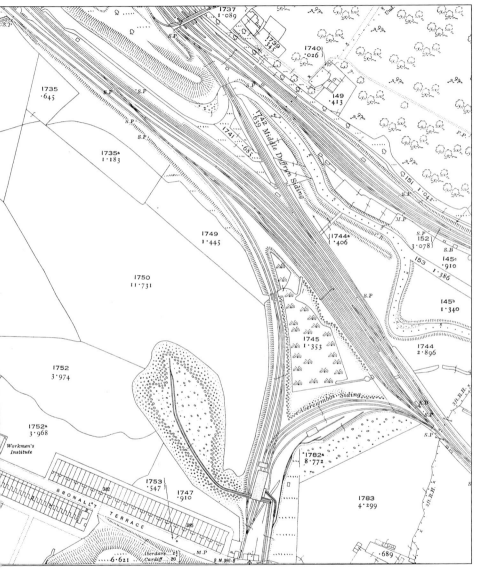

Middle Duffryn Sidings was the main point of connection from the GWR (top right) to the TVR. Also shown on this map is the Powell Duffryn Railway coming from top left to a junction with the TVR line bottom right, and the separate PD branch to Abercwmboi Colliery and siding. *Reproduced from the 25", 1919 Ordnance Survey Map*

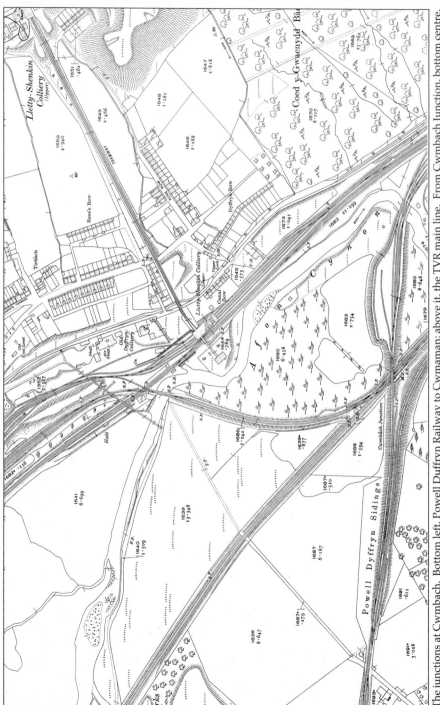

The junctions at Cwmbach. Bottom left, Powell Duffryn Railway to Cwmaman; above it, the TVR main line. From Cwmbach Junction, bottom centre, the TVR Cwmbach branch runs across the GWR main line to join the Abernant Railway. The Lletty Shenkin colliery line originally joined the TVR at Cwmbach Junction. *Reproduced from the 25″, 1919 Ordnance Survey Map*

pm, but was over ½ hour late due to the earlier part of the tour getting behind schedule.

The Taff Vale Royal Train consisted of 'C' class 4-4-2T No. 173 suitably decorated for the occasion, one six-wheeled brake van, one composite bogie carriage and the Directors' bogie saloon, and was accompanied by Mr Ammon Beasley, the TVR General Manager, throughout. The Royal party was attended by Lord Merthyr during the tour of the valleys.

Aberdare station was at last renewed during 1913 and 1914 (BoT Inspection 21st April, 1914), red brick building, standard for the Taff in the early years of the century, being put up on the site of the old station. At last the principal station on the branch, and one of the TVR's more important stations, was worthy of the town in which it was built. Plans were completed early in 1912, these being approved by the Board of Trade Inspector at a site visit on 16th April, 1912. Contracts were let and demolition of the old station and construction of the new station started early in 1913. As previously stated, the steam railcar service beyond Aberdare station was closed as from 1st June, 1912, and Aberdare again became the terminal station for all branch passenger services, apart from the colliers' trains into the Dare Valley.

Beyond Mill Street, Ysguborwen Colliery (often spelt Sguborwen) had had a shaky existence for many years. It had been closed at the end of 1895, but re-opened again in September 1906, only to close again in August 1908. The last traffic cleared by the Taff Vale Railway from the colliery was on 27th August of that year. The following year the colliery was acquired by the Powell Duffryn Company and not finally abandoned until August 1919, but the branch to the Taff Vale line at Mill Street was never re-opened. It was taken up and the bridge over the River Cynon removed.

The bridge across the Cynon river linking Navigation Colliery with the TVR sidings at Mountain Ash; the GWR station is at the left.   *Lens of Sutton*

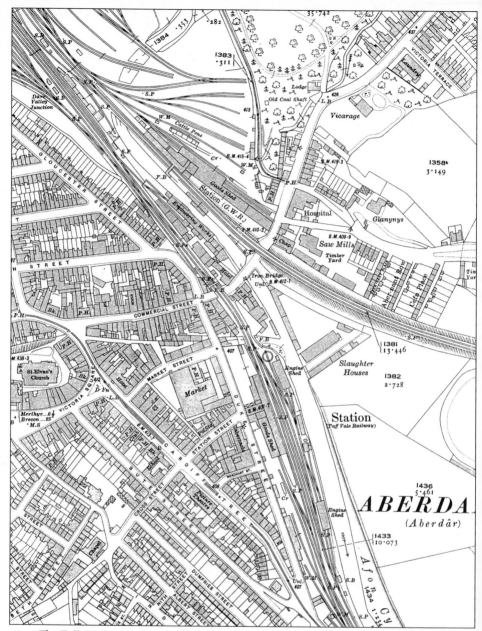

The Taff Vale Railway station at Aberdare in 1919, showing the two locomotive sheds; note how it is constricted by the Cynon river immediately adjacent to the east. Dare Valley Junction, top left, was where the branch to Bwllfa Dare started. The GWR High Level station is just beyond the top left. The line along the street east of the GWR sidings is the old Aberdare-Hirwain Tramroad still in place in part.

Reproduced from the 25", 1919 Ordnance Survey Map

Chapter Seven

The GWR Takes Over

With traffic on the wane after World War I, coupled with a serious drop in tonnage due to the 1921 Coal Strike, the scene was set for the great railway amalgamation schemes which followed the passing of the Railways Act on 19th August, 1921. The Taff Vale Railway was amalgamated with the GWR under the GWR (Western Group) Preliminary Amalgamation Scheme of 25th March, 1922, backdated to 1st January for accountancy purposes.

The first outward sign in the valley of the amalgamation was the appearance of GWR 0-6-0 pannier and saddle tanks on some coal trains in 1923. The railmotor Platforms on the main line, Abercwmboi, Mathewstown and Pontcynon Bridge were re-named Halts, to conform with GWR standard practice, with the Winter issue of the GWR public timetable dated 2nd October, 1922, although no public announcement appears to have been made. The Platform at Mill Street, and those on the Dare Valley branch used exclusively for colliers' trains remained as Platforms in the Working Timetables, in fact those on the Dare branch always remained so until closure in 1949. Mill Street Platform was closed at the end of 1924. Towards the end of 1927 the former Taff Vale engine shed, alongside Aberdare station, was closed and the engines and men transferred to the GWR shed, a new direct connection from the TVR line being put in immediately west of the crossing gates, thence across the GWR line to the shed sidings at Robertstown.

The GWR line became known as the High Level line and the former TVR the Low Level line. From 1st July, 1924 the main stations on the line were re-named to avoid any confusion. The former Taff stations at Aberdare and Penrhiwceiber had 'Low Level' added to the names, whilst Mountain Ash TVR station became Mountain Ash (Oxford Street). One further change of name took place, much later, when Pontcynon Bridge Halt was shortened to Pontcynon Halt, as from 8th June, 1953.

One further early result of the amalgamation was the closure of the short spur from the GWR line at Gadlys Junction, which crossed the TVR line on the level before entering Gadlys Colliery and Brickworks. This was taken up about 1925, the traffic afterwards being catered for by the existing former TVR sidings.

The General Strike of 1926 marked the beginning of the slump in the coal trade from which the valley never recovered. Demand for steam coal considerably reduced with the rapid development of the internal combustion engine, and the Aberdare valley - and the other steam coal producing valleys in South Wales - became a very depressed area, with unemployment or short time working the order of the day.

As previously recorded the Cwmbach branch closed at the end of 1935, the traffic from River Level colliery passing on to the GWR High Level line via Cwmbach sidings. This lasted only a short time, however, as the colliery closed early in 1940. The rail level crossing of the Cwmbach branch over the GWR line

Most TVR engines were 'Great Westernised' to some extent; 'O4' class No. 39 seen above has received the full treatment when photographed in 1940. *W. Leslie Good*

The junction at Pontcynon in 1962 with the Nixon's private railway, curving right towards Navigation Colliery. *M. Hale/ C. Chapman Collection*

was taken out, and for the first time since 1856 the GWR line was free of hindrance. The bridge carrying the Cwmbach branch over the River Cynon was also removed, but the remainder of the branch from the south bank of the river to Cwmbach Junction was retained as a siding. This was eventually closed as from 1st June, 1957 and the sidings were taken up. The section of the branch north of the river was sold to the Aberdare UDC in May 1961 for industrial development.

On a reduced scale coal traffic still continued in the later 1930s. There was still a fair amount of traffic from the Powell Duffryn collieries in the Aman Valley, Nixon's collieries in the Mountain Ash area, also from Penrikyber Colliery, (note new spelling). This continued through World War II, but demand rapidly declined afterwards and further colliery closures followed the formation of the National Coal Board in 1947. On the brighter side the Powell Duffryn Company had started a huge phurnacite patent fuel plant at Abercwmboi in 1937, and this was in full production by 1942, one of the most impressive sights in the valley.

Colliery closures restarted with Cwmnoel, in the lower Aman Valley, in 1948, and Nantmelyn (Bwllfa No. 2) in the Dare Valley in 1956. The only production left in the Aberdare area itself after that was from Aberaman and Fforchaman, both former Powell Duffryn pits in the Aman Valley area. Aberaman was the first of these to go, closing in 1962, Fforchaman following three years later. After that mineral traffic from the top of the Aberdare valley was confined to coal from Tower Colliery at Hirwaun, and stone ballast from the Penderyn Quarry, also near Hirwaun. This was conveyed to the former Taff Vale line via the old Vale of Neath section of the GWR, crossing over to the Low Level line at Gadlys Junction.

Down the lower end of the Aberdare Valley Nixon's Navigation Colliery which, along with the other Nixon collieries in the area, had been taken over by the Powell Duffryn Company in 1936, was closed as an independent concern late in 1940, but was retained both in conjunction with nearby Deep Duffryn Colliery and for maintenance purposes. Still further eastwards down the valley, Cwmcynon Colliery closed early in 1949. Growth of light industries at Hirwaun and in the Robertstown area of Aberdare had little effect on the rapidly declining traffic on the former Taff Vale branch; both were closer to the High Level line, although road transport catered for most of the traffic from these sources anyway. Similarly the trading estate development at Ynysboeth, at the lower end of the valley, is covered by road transport.

On the passenger side, the introduction of motor buses saw a marked decline in passenger receipts in the 1920s, this further deteriorated during the depression years of the 1930s. Despite this, the GWR had improved the branch service from the 12 trains each weekday in 1922, when it had taken over, to 15 in 1927 and 17 (average) immediately before the War, in 1939. Precise figures for the period are not quoted as several trains operated on certain days of the week only. During World War II the service was curtailed to essential services only; in 1942 there were 11 trains plus a workmen's and a railmotor (one class) working. After the War the service was again improved to reach a peak of well

Mathewstown Platform, between Abercynon and Penrhiwceiber, looking up the valley in 1971, seven years after closing.   *Oakwood Collection*

Penrhiwceiber Low Level station, looking towards Abercynon.   *C. Chapman Collection*

Penrhiwceiber Low Level station in 1959, looking towards Aberdare.   *H.C. Casserley*

Mountain Ash station looking down the valley in 1959, with Navigation Colliery on the left; the disused Abergorki d colliery is in the background.   *M. Hale/ C. Chapman Collection*

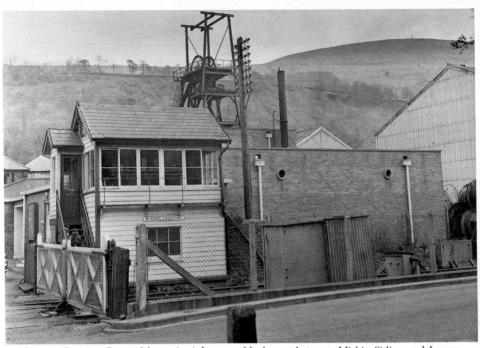

Nixons Crossing Box at Mountain Ash was a block post between Miskin Siding and Lower Duffryn boxes.   *Welsh Industrial & Maritime Museum*

Outside the locomotive shed at Mountain Ash NCB; on the right is Sir John (Avonside 1680 of 1914); on the left, No. 8 (Robert Stephenson of 1944).   *Oakwood Collection*

over 20 trains each way daily as from 21st September, 1953. This included an hourly regular interval auto-train service on the branch, with a few ordinary trains, some to/from Cardiff, sandwiched in between at peak hours.

Despite this passenger receipts declined, for although the main stations at Aberdare and Mountain Ash were well sited, the buses were running through the whole ribbon development of housing in the valley, and captured the vast majority of the local traffic. Abercwmboi Halt was not well sited to modern needs, and few of the auto-trains stopped there in later years. It was finally closed as from 2nd April, 1956. With the demand gone, the passenger service was drastically reduced in 1962, except on Saturdays when 18 up and 16 down trains were run. Finally in 1963 the service was proposed for closure in Dr Beeching's 'Reshaping of British Railways' report, and closure notices were published.

After the customary objections the last passenger trains were run on the branch on Saturday 14th March, 1964, official closure being as from the following Monday. As from that date the stations at Aberdare (Low Level), Aberaman, Mountain Ash (Oxford Street) and Penrhiwceiber (Low Level) were closed completely, as goods traffic, apart from private sidings traffic, had been withdrawn from the other stations as from 2nd December, 1963. Goods traffic was withdrawn from Aberdare (Low Level) as from 3rd August, 1964, and with it came the complete closure of the station. Most of the station buildings on the branch were demolished during 1968/9, although Mountain Ash (Oxford Street) went earlier than the others as part of the up platform was sold to an adjacent business concern.

Following cessation of passenger services the branch remained more or less intact for a further four years, although Middle Duffryn sidings were taken out of active use following the closure of Fforchaman Colliery in 1965. The branch was singled from Abercynon North to the terminus as from Monday 16th November, 1968, when the signal boxes at Pontcynon Junction, Penrhiwceiber Upper, Penrhiwceiber Lower, Nixon's Crossing, Cwmbach Junction and Aberaman were taken out of use. Of these the original McKenzie & Holland box still existed at Pontcynon Junction, complete with its elaborate end barge boarding and wooden TVR name plate. The only boxes on the branch open by 1973 were at Abercwmboi, the junction for the sidings to the Phurnacite Plant (closed in March 1990), and at Aberdare North to cover the road level crossing gates. At the lower end of the branch Abercynon Station signal box, on the former TVR main line, controlled the junction to the branch. The passenger line connection at the north end of the station was taken out, only the mineral line connection south of the signal box and station remaining.

The old up main line was chiefly used for the single line, but did cross over to the old down main line here and there, particularly between Deep Duffryn and Middle Duffryn. The branch was divided into two single line sections, Abercynon to Abercwmboi, and Abercwmboi to Aberdare North, each controlled by Electric Token, the section between Aberdare North and Aberdare High Level, i.e. the GWR-built connection with the former Vale of Neath line, being under signalman's and foreman's control. The old Taff Vale line became the only rail exit from the Aberdare Valley and the Hirwaun area, the former GWR line being cut at Hirwaun Pond at one end, and Cresselley Crossing at Mountain Ash the other end. The latter was soon shortened to Mountain Ash West, and in 1971 back to Cwmbach, ready for a new crossover to the TVR line. The remaining section of the old High Level line, i.e. from Hirwaun Pond to Cwmbach, was now classed as a siding.

Three National Coal Board (NCB) private sidings were listed on the former TVR line in early 1972, namely those at Abercwmboi for the phurnacite plant, Mountain Ash for the Aberdare Valley Central Washery (AVCW) and at Penrikyber Colliery. In addition, by this time accessible only via the TVR line, there were, on the former Vale of Neath section, NCB sidings at Aberdare for Robertstown Opencast, and at Hirwaun for Tower Colliery. Aberdare High Level yard was open for public freight traffic, including domestic coal.

There was a possibility that if Tower Colliery at Hirwaun closed, there would be no purpose in maintaining a railway westward from Abercwmboi.

When the future of Tower Colliery had been assured, moves were put afoot to link the Vale of Neath and TVR lines in the Cwmbach area, and dispense with the TVR line westward thereof, so releasing land sought by the Aberdare Urban District Council for road improvements, and enabling the long awaited closure of the troublesome Commercial Street level crossing by the former Aberdare Low Level station.

The link between the TVR and Vale of Neath lines involved crossing the River Cynon, and for this purpose a 110 yds-long steel girder span was used which had formerly carried the Princes Risborough-Oxford line over the A40 near Wheatley.

Abercwmboi Halt, looking towards Aberdare; the 'staggered' platforms were extremely short.   *B.J. Miller Collection*

Abercwmboi signal box, looking north in 1989, with the now closed colliery beyond.

R.W. Ranson

From Aberaman station, looking towards Abercynon, in August 1958; on the right is the Treaman Siding and the private Powell Duffryn Railway down the Aman Valley.

M. Hale/ C. Chapman Collection

The connection at Aberdare by which in GWR days former TVR engines were able to use the GWR engine sheds.

M. Hale/ C. Chapman Collection

A train of empties southbound in charge of diesel locomotive No, 6971 passing Deep Duffryn Colliery in May 1973; this colliery did not close until 1980.   *Tom Heavyside*

In May 1973 a train of ballast from Penderyn Quarries runs down the valley past the Aberaman Phurnacite works in the background; the three quarries at Penderyn north of Hirwain had used the former GWR line until it was closed.   *Tom Heavyside*

The ceremony on 11th August, 1973, to mark the opening of the new connection at Cwmbach; Cardiff Divisional Manager E.R. Williams, with the Mayor and Clerk, and the MP for Aberdare.   *British Rail*

The new connecting line diverges from the ex-TVR line alignment at 22 miles 01 chains (measured from Cardiff, Bute Road), just west of the Abercwmboi network of sidings, and includes a gradient of 1 in 84 (climbing in the up direction), in addition to the river bridge. 12,000 tons of ballast were brought to the site to provide the necessary levels for the line. At 22 miles 23 chains the mileage changes to 20 miles 68 chains, measured from Pontypool Road, as the former Vale of Neath line is joined. At this end of the connection the shortening and raising of a footbridge was necessary. From Cwmbach to Aberdare High Level the Vale of Neath line reverted from siding to running line status.

The 1¾ miles former trackbed of the TVR line westwards from Cwmbach was eventually occupied principally by a new main road approach to Aberdare, the present A4059, the main objective of the District Council funding the £120,000 cost of the new rail connection.

Since 1971, excursion trains had operated from Aberdare High Level, where they used the former westbound platform. Departing trains backed out of the station towards Robertstown, and then reversed to proceed over the connection to the ex-TVR line. Before reaching Abercynon, the trains also picked up passengers at Penrhiwceiber. Such trains ran either to a specified destination, or were part of the then popular programme of 'Mystery Excursions' from South Wales. A typical 'Mystery' in April 1973 left Aberdare H.L. at 8.00 am, and Penrhiwceiber at 8.30 am, being due back at 10.36 pm (Penrhiwceiber) and 11.10 pm (Aberdare), at a cost of £1.50, or 80p for children under 14. Tickets were sold by BR ticket agents in Aberdare and Mountain Ash, and, by post if necessary, by the BR Area Manager at Pontypridd.

A departing excursion from Aberdare to Brighton on Sunday 29th July, 1973, was the last train to use the Aberdare connection between the V of N and TVR lines and to cross the Commercial Street crossing. While the train was away, the new Cwmbach connecting line was brought into use, and the return excursion, arriving in the early hours of Monday 30th July was the first revenue earning train over it.

An official opening ceremony of the new line was conducted on Friday 10th August, 1973, when a tape was cut on the bridge by Councillor E.D. Jenkins, Chairman of Aberdare Urban District Council. He, and other guests, were brought to the bridge from Aberdare H.L. in a special train formed of a class '37' diesel-electric locomotive and the Western Region General Manager's Saloon, the BR officers on board being headed by Mr E.R. Williams, divisional manager for South Wales. After the ceremony the train proceeded the length of the Cynon Valley line in both directions, going first to Abercynon, and then back to Hirwaun, before returning the guests to Aberdare.

Another important event in 1973, and one indicative of the significance of freight traffic in the Cynon Valley at the time, was the selection of the Aberdare area (along with Radyr) for the first field trials on BR Western Region of the Total Operations Processing System (TOPS). This system, which eventually covered the entire BR network in 1975, monitors in 'real time' the movement of freight rolling stock - the system was subsequently extended to locomotives and passenger vehicles - to improve utilisation and transits, and to provide vital

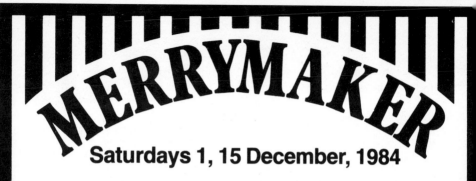

MERRYMAKER

Saturdays 1, 15 December, 1984

Special train service from
Aberdare and Mountain Ash to

PONTYPRIDD and CARDIFF

for shopping, football, visiting friends etc.

Aberdare	d	09 40	12 40	15 40
Mountain Ash	d	10 00	13 00	16 00
Pontypridd	a	10 27	13 27	16 27
Cardiff Queen Street	a	10 52	13 52	16 52
Cardiff Central	a	10 57	13 57	16 57
Cardiff Central	d	11 12	14 12	17 12
Cardiff Queen Street	d	11 16	14 16	17 16
Pontypridd	d	11 43	14 43	17 43
Mountain Ash	d	12 15	15 15	18 15
Aberdare	a	12 30	15 30	18 30

Day Return Fare

Aberdare ⎫
Mountain Ash ⎭ to Pontypridd **£1**   Cardiff **£2**

Aberdare to Mountain Ash   **50p**

Children 5 and under 16 years ⎫ half-fare
Railcard holders ⎭

Published by British Rail Western   PSC 8949/1112

Mid Glamorgan
COUNTY COUNCIL

This is the age of the train ⫸

management information.

A Royal Train operated over the line from Abercynon on the morning of Saturday 10th September, 1977, when HRH The Prince of Wales arrived after an overnight journey from Scotland to open the South Wales Motor Show in Aberdare. The train utilised the High Level 'westbound' platform, as used by the excursion trains already referred to. These latter trains continued until 1980, when they were discontinued for a while to permit economies in track maintenance, although by then they had ceased to call at Penrhiwceiber because of the deterioration of the platform there, but the trains were picking up at Mountain Ash where it had been found possible, subject to certain safety measures, to utilise a narrow part of the former 'up' platform left after most of the Oxford Street station site had been given over to commercial development.

At the time of the opening of the new link at Cwmbach in 1973, there was speculation about passenger services being restored, BR's stance being preparedness to operate such services provided any capital outlay or running loss were met by the new Mid-Glamorgan County Council under the powers they would assume when taking over in 1974.

By 1981, Penrikyber Colliery, AVCW washery at Mountain Ash, Abercwmboi Phurnacite Plant, and (on the V of N section) Tower Colliery at Hirwaun were still listed as rail terminals, along with Aberdare High Level goods yard and the Penderyn ballast connection at Hirwaun. The train plan in force just prior to the start of the year-long miners' strike in 1984 served Penrikyber Colliery (1,000 tonnes per week to Abercwmboi), Abercwmboi Phurnacite Plant (18,000 tonnes inwards per week, 8,000 tonnes outwards) and Tower Colliery (1,500 tonnes outwards per week to Abercwmboi). No provision was made for the new Cwm Cynon Tip coal disposal point at Penrhiwceiber, on the north side of the line (although Merry-go-round 'MGR' trains to Aberthaw power station resumed after the strike).

So far as other traffic is concerned, Aberdare High Level yard had ceased to cater for general public traffic in May 1982, and in 1984 domestic coal traffic was to cease as well. For a time, however, brick traffic was handled at Aberdare, conveyed by the 'Speedlink' air-braked wagon-load service (which finished, nationally, in 1991). In 1984, ballast trains from Hirwaun (Penderyn) were provided for on an 'as required' basis, and are recorded as ceasing finally in 1985. Another casualty of 1985 was Penrikyber Colliery which closed in October that year in the immediate aftermath of the miners' strike.

Chronologically it is appropriate to mention here, although not strictly on 'Aberdare Railway' territory, that the former goods shed of wooden construction at Aberdare High Level, and attributed to I.K. Brunel through his connections with the Vale of Neath Railway, was burnt down on 7th November, 1982.

The emergence of 'Sector' management on BR in the early 1980s led to closer focus on the problems of 'grant-aided' passenger services, i.e. those supported by the government Passenger Obligation Grant, such as the services radiating from Cardiff to the Valleys, i.e. to Treherbert (Rhondda), Merthyr (passing through Abercynon and the junction with the Aberdare line) and Rhymney.

A Christmas shoppers' special for Cardiff at the re-opened Aberdare High Level platform on 1st December, 1984, photographed from the Hirwain end.   *D.K. Lewis*

A 'Sprinter' No. 150 263 breasts a ceremonial tape at Abercynon North on re-opening day, 27th September, 1988.

Improvements to services, and selective fare reductions, both introduced by BR in 1983/4 on these routes, coupled with the opening of the county council funded station at Cathays, Cardiff, in October 1983, led to increased patronage of the trains.

As a 'toe in the water' exercise to test the potential for passenger trains in the Cynon Valley, BR operated special trains from Aberdare and Mountain Ash to Pontypridd and Cardiff on two pre-Christmas Saturdays in 1984, on 1st and 15th December. Each of the three trains in each direction was formed of two 3-car class '116' diesel multiple unit sets, normally out of use on Saturdays. £2 return was charged to Cardiff, and over 1,000 passengers were carried on the first day, twice the number expected, and ensuring that similar specials operated periodically thereafter, for example on Saturday 16th February and 16th March, 1985, mainly for sporting events, while examples in 1986 are a three train Saturday service throughout the summer, and trains on Mondays to Fridays during the two peak holiday weeks, 21st July to 1st August. Speed restrictions due to track conditions and signalling requirements on the Aberdare branch, led to the passenger trains between Aberdare and Cardiff at this time taking approximately 1¼ hours for the journey.

In September 1985, Mid and South Glamorgan county councils published a Rail Development Strategy for the Valley lines. This proposed a £5.2 million investment programme by the counties, alongside BR's proposal to introduce new-generation diesel multiple units and further service improvements, the programme having the support of the Welsh Office as a 'Project of Regional or National Importance'. The programme included £2 million for re-opening the Aberdare passenger service, namely £450,000 for stations, £700,000 for signalling and telecommunications, £250,000 for track improvements and £600,000 for a class '150/2' 'Sprinter' dmu, these costs to be met by Mid Glamorgan County Council, with some funding eventually coming from the European Regional Development Fund.

Operating costs of the service were to be borne by BR, who would also retain the receipts from fares. An operating loss was forecast for the first year, when the service would operate at a reduced frequency, with a break-even situation, and operating profit thereafter. The service was to be introduced under the provisions of the 'Speller Act', i.e. a new Section 56A added in 1981 to the Transport Act of 1962 whereby train services can be introduced on an experimental basis and, if found unsuccessful, the services can be withdrawn without going through the normal lengthy closure-of-lines procedure. Being experimental, the service was not supported by the Passenger Service Obligation Grant from central government, as enjoyed by other services, and all BR costs had to be met from income.

An agreement to proceed with the project was signed between Mid Glamorgan County Council and British Rail on 28th March, 1988, with an official 'start-of-work' ceremony the following day, although some preparatory work was already in hand by that time.

New stations, each comprising a 49-metre platform and principal shelter were provided at Abercynon North, Penrhiwceiber, Mountain Ash, Fernhill,

Cwmbach and Aberdare. Abercynon North (16 miles 40 chains from Cardiff Bute Road) is just west of the original Abercynon station, renamed Abercynon South. The running line to Aberdare no longer ran alongside the platform at Abercynon (South) and therefore a new platform was necessary, and its location is close to the town centre and enables a small 'park-and-ride' car park to be provided. Penrhiwceiber is at the site of the former Low Level station (18 m. 75 ch.), while Mountain Ash (20 m. 05 ch. is slightly to the east of the former Oxford Street station where as mentioned earlier, platform width was restricted. The new station site at Mountain Ash also has 'park-and-ride' facilities.

Fernhill (20 m. 78 ch.) is just east of the Abercwmboi complex of lines; Cwmbach (20 m. 72 ch. - measured from Pontypool Road) is just beyond the western end of the 1973 connection to the Vale of Neath line, and realignment of a curve here to increase line speed from 10 mph to 30 mph necessitated removal of the footbridge which had been altered to accommodate the 1973 link. Cwmbach is the only station to have its platform on the north or down side of the line: the other five are on the south or up side.

At Aberdare (22 m. 34 ch.) the platform is virtually on the site of the former High Level westbound platform, but the track has been slewed and raised. Park-and-ride facilities are nearby, and a bus bay is provided for the Rail Link bus service to Penywaun, Hirwaun and Rhigos. After the inauguration of the passenger service, a ticket office was added at Aberdare, which is staffed in the mornings: otherwise tickets are issued on the train by conductors.

The official opening of the Aberdare passenger service took place on Tuesday morning, 27th September, 1988, when guests joined a special class '150/2' 'Sprinter' at Pontypridd for an all-stations run to Aberdare, with brief opening ceremonies at each stop. At Abercynon North the train was driven through a tape to inaugurate the new service, while the main opening was at Aberdare, where James Knapp, General Secretary of the National Union of Railwaymen declared the service open and unveiled a plaque.

The names of three stations require bi-lingual presentation. These are Abercynon North/Gogledd, Mountain Ash/Aberpennar and Aberdare/ Aberdar.

On Sunday 2nd October, an introductory service operated between Pontypridd and Aberdare (with the first up service originating, and the final down service terminating, at Cardiff Central) with passengers carried free, prior to the service proper commencing the following day. A basic two-hourly service operated on Mondays to Fridays, hourly on Saturdays. On the first Saturday, 8th October a flat fare of 50p applied on the Aberdare line, with special attractions in Aberdare town itself.

A more frequent service on Mondays to Fridays required increased track capacity, bearing in mind that an unbroken single line section applied for the five miles between Abercynon and Abercwmboi, and that the existing freight services had to be accommodated on Mondays to Fridays in addition to new passenger trains. Another requirement for a more frequent passenger service on Mondays to Fridays was the availability of an additional class '150/2'

'Sprinter' unit, the funding of which was being provided by Mid Glamorgan County Council.

These obstacles were overcome for the winter 1989/90 service, since when, an hourly passenger service has operated on the Aberdare line on Mondays to Saturdays. The 'Sprinter' unit funded by the county council was No. 150 282, while new signalling was brought into use on Monday 9th October, 1989. This provides track circuit block working with colour light signals (except for semaphore signals retained at Abercynon) between Abercynon and Aberdare, with a passing loop at Abercwmboi, all controlled from a VDU mini-panel in Abercynon signal box. At Abercwmboi the former up loop became the main bi-directional running line, with the former down loop being retained for passenger purposes. Intermediate colour light signals in the Penrhiwceiber area, coupled with axle counters, divide the Abercynon-Abercwmboi section into two, enabling both freight trains and an hourly passenger service to be run. In the new signalling the run-round loop at Penrhiwceiber and the connection to Cwm Cynon tip were retained, also connections into the phurnacite plant at Aberdare. Abercwmboi signal box, an ex-TVR structure, was closed.

The Abercynon signalman is also responsible for movements at Aberdare west of the passenger station, with 'One Train Working' applying on the line on to Tower Colliery at Hirwaun.

At this juncture the passenger services were the responsibility of the 'Provincial Services' Sector of British Rail, which was to be renamed Regional Railways in December 1990, while Railfreight Coal was the operator of freight services.

Ironically, as the new signalling and increased capacity came into being, events were unfolding which were to lead to reduced freight activity on the Aberdare line. In late 1988 'Merry-go-round' operation of coal trains from Tower Colliery to Abercwmboi and Aberthaw power station began, and in the following year containerised movements of long distance coal for shipping to Northern Ireland commenced. Both these measures, though increasing train loads and efficiency, reduced train movements. Then in late 1989 Merthyr Vale Colliery in the adjacent Taff Valley which had supplied coal to Abercwmboi in trains running via Abercynon and reversing in the former Stormstown yard, closed. Maerdy Colliery in the Rhondda Fach another source of fuel for Abercwmboi, had closed earlier. One result of these changes was the closure of Aberdare train crew depot and locomotive stabling point in October 1989.

Then in March 1990 the Abercwmboi phurnacite plant closed: although this closure was greeted by those who deplored the caustic environmental pollution from the plant, it inevitably led to loss of jobs for local people. The last two coke ovens closed on 22nd March, 1990, with the last MGR train from Tower Colliery recorded the previous day. All MGR wagons were reported cleared from Abercwmboi by the end of the month, although containerised output, together with products from the plant for domestic fuel depots, are said to have continued for some months.

So far as freight traffic on the Aberdare line was concerned, this left Tower Colliery at Hirwaun as the only source, generating mainly power station coal

The new layout at Abercynon; the Merthyr line is on the right, passing the former station house; Aberdare trains use Abercynon North, the platform on the curve at the left; the photographer is standing at the end of the new Abercynon South; June 1989.   *David Gould*

A steam special from Cardiff on 27th October, 1991, showing the bridge built to connect the low and high level lines at Cwmbach; preserved 2-6-4T No. 80080 is hauling stock in Network South-East livery.   *R.W. Ranson*

for Aberthaw, near Barry, in MGR trains, and some containerised shipment traffic. Furthermore, Tower was destined to be the final deep mine to be operational in the entire, once vast, South Wales coalfield, while the MGR trains from the pit were to be the last to fulfill the original coal-conveying purpose of the Taff Vale Railway, and, bound for Aberthaw, they ran on ex-TVR metals through Cogan Junction, close to the former TVR sponsored docks at Penarth.

In 1991 celebrations were conducted to mark the 150th anniversary of the opening throughout of the Taff Vale Railway from Merthyr to Cardiff in 1841. Known as the 'TVR150' events, these included some special steam-hauled passenger trains, hauled by privately-owned BR Standard class '4' 2-6-4T No. 80080. A series of proving runs were held on Sunday 29th September, 1991 when the load was a support coach, and two 2-car class '116' dmu sets, in which seats were available to rail staff. The runs this day included a 3.08 pm Cardiff Central-Aberdare and 4.50 pm return, both calling at Pontypridd and routed via Llandaff. No. 80080 ran bunker-first on the 'down' run to Cardiff. On Sunday 27th October 1991, the final day of the runs for the general public, the load was five Network South East coaches, the 10.53 am trip from Cardiff Central ran to Aberdare via the Cardiff 'City Line', i.e. via Fairwater, returning at 12.40 pm (via Llandaff). Again the 27th October runs also called at Pontypridd.

A Sunday service to and from Aberdare was operated during the winter timetable 1989/90, and has been provided summer and winter since then with the exception of winter 1990/1.

British Coal proposed the closure of Tower Colliery in 1994 with the production ceasing on 15th April. Large ground stocks remained and rail movements continued until November 1994. Later the management and employees of Tower Colliery purchased the pit and took possession on 2nd January, 1995. As this book goes to press, output from the colliery is being blended nearby in another valley (being taken there by road) before being loaded onto rail, but there is the prospect of trains resuming from Tower itself in the future.

The freight trains have been operated, since the pre-privatisation break-up of British Rail on 1st April, 1994 by the Transrail Company. At the same time infrastructure and signalling were passed to Railtrack, and passenger trains operated by the Cardiff Valleys Train Operating Unit (TOU) of BR, using trains now belonging to and leased from the Porterbrook Leasing Company, and leasing stations from Railtrack. The dmu fleet leased to the TOU as a whole was 14 class '143' 'Pacer' units and 17 class '150/2' 'Sprinter' units.

In April 1995 the Cardiff Railway Company was vested to take over the operations of the TOU.

The Aberdare passenger service has confidently passed through its first five experimental years, 1988-1993, and, along with the other Cardiff Valleys services, will eventually be offered for franchise to the private sector.

An early photograph of the tiny Abercwmboi Platform looking down towards Abercynon.

Lens of Sutton

Aberaman station with a down-valley train of six-wheeled stock.

Lens of Sutton

Chapter Eight

Train Services

Passenger Train Services

When the Aberdare Railway opened in August 1846, it provided a service of three trains each way on weekdays and two each way on Sundays. All trains catered for first, second and third class passengers, and conveniently connected at Navigation House with both up and down trains on the Taff Vale Railway main line. Thus passengers from either Cardiff or Merthyr direction had immediate connection with the Aberdare valley trains, and the valley passengers had similar connection to all stations on the TVR line. The opening timetable for the Aberdare Railway is set out below:

	Weekdays			*Sundays*	
	am	*pm*	*pm*	*am*	*pm*
Aberdare	9.15	1.30	5.30	9.15	2.15
Mountain Ash	9.30	1.45	5.45	9.30	2.30
Navigation House	9.45	2.00	6.00	9.45	2.45
Navigation House	9.55	2.10	6.10	9.55	2.55
Mountain Ash	10.10	2.25	6.25	10.10	3.10
Aberdare	10.25	2.40	6.40	10.25	3.25

Through tickets were available to or from any station on the Taff Vale line, although at the start only single tickets were issued on weekdays. To encourage Sunday travel return tickets, then called 'To and Fro' tickets, were issued at single fare for the return journey. Specimen fares, from Cardiff, at the opening are given below, and these remained practically unaltered for the next 50 years, although by that time return fares had been slightly reduced, and numerous other cheap rate tickets were available.

	Single Fares from Cardiff to:		
	Navigation House	*Mountain Ash*	*Aberdare*
First Class	2s. 8d.	3s. 8d.	4s. 0d.
Second Class	2s. 0d.	2s. 8d.	3s. 0d.
Third Class	1s. 4d.	1s. 8d.	2s. 0d.

Considering the average working man in the Aberdare area was receiving about £1 per week in wages, some much less, a day out in Cardiff for a man and his family must have been a rare luxury in those days.

An extra train was usually put on at Bank Holidays, but the first recorded excursions by the TVR from Aberdare were on Monday 9th August, 1847 when two specials were run, one at 8.30 am, the other at 3 pm, to Cardiff to witness the ascent of Mr C. Green's Balloon 'The Royal Sovereign'.

Apart from minor alterations of train times, the basic service remained unchanged until 13th April, 1848 when an early morning train was added, both on the Taff main line and the Aberdare branch. By that time, of course, stations had been added at both Aberdare Mill Street, which became the new terminus, and at Aberaman. Treaman station was added later in 1848. The extra train left Mill Street at 6.50 am and arrived at Navigation House at 7.30; the connecting train reached Cardiff at 8.40. Sunday services remained unaltered and the fourth train must have proved unremunerative, as it was withdrawn at the end of August of the same year.

The next changes took place on the main line early the following year when the train times were altered, and the up and down trains no longer crossed at Navigation House (renamed Aberdare Junction in 1849). This made connections between the Aberdare branch and main line trains inconvenient, to put it mildly. This applied to both weekdays and Sunday trains, and led to such complaints that for a while, from 1st May, 1849, five trains each way were run on weekdays on the branch, and four on Sundays. This was one of the rare occasions in the 19th century when the local service was far better than on the main line. Of the five trains, however, three connected at Aberdare Junction with trains to Cardiff, and the other two with Merthyr trains, no connection being made with the early afternoon up train to Merthyr. This extraordinary service on the branch lasted a fortnight only, after which the service was cut back to four each way on weekdays and three each way on Sundays, some of the three trains running on the main line being retimed to give better connections.

This arrangement lasted until Monday 29th July, 1850 when the branch service reverted to three trains on weekdays and two on Sundays, as the main line timetable had remained throughout. The weekday connections to and from Cardiff were excellent, but connection to Merthyr was virtually non-existent. This strange state of affairs was due to the down main line trains arriving at Aberdare Junction between one and a quarter and two hours before the up trains. The branch trains arrived in convenient time to connect with the down trains, and remained at Aberdare Junction for the up train to arrive. Any unfortunate passenger who wished to go from any of the stations on the branch to Merthyr, just had to wait with it. Again complaints were made and, on Monday 2nd September, 1850, a fourth train was added to the branch service to connect with the first up Merthyr train of the day, but nothing was done about the other two up trains.

No further alteration was made for over 12 months and it was not until Monday 17th November, 1851 that the TVR completely retimed their main line services so that up and down trains again crossed at Aberdare Junction, thus allowing the branch service to return to the basic three trains each way. The Sunday service of two trains remained as before.

One interesting excursion was run from Aberdare on 18th August, 1851, in connection with the Great Exhibition held at Crystal Palace. This left at 5 am and connected with a similar excursion from Merthyr. On arrival at Cardiff the passengers had to walk over to the South Wales Railway station to join a broad gauge excursion to Paddington. As the bridge over the River Wye at Chepstow, which would allow through rail travel from South Wales to London, was still under construction at the time, the route had to be by SWR train to Newport, thence by vessel of the Screw Steam Packet Company across the Bristol Channel to Bristol, and finally by GWR broad gauge train to Paddington.

The service of three trains each way on weekdays remained unaltered for a further 12 years, and frequently the retiming of trains on the main line resulted in very poor connections from the branch trains, at Aberdare Junction, with the main line trains to Merthyr. This did not cause too much inconvenience as an alternative route to Merthyr had been started by the Vale of Neath Railway, first by horse bus from Merthyr Road Station (near Aberdare) as from 24th September, 1851, and then by rail, either via Hirwain or from Llwydcoed, as from 2nd November, 1853. For people living in the Aberdare area the Vale of Neath's route was more direct.

It was also during this period that the first closure of passenger stations took place. Mill Street was the first to go, as from 22nd November, 1852, Aberdare station once again becoming the passenger terminus on the branch. The other to disappear in the 1850s was Aberaman (Saturday 12th July, 1856), but as this was more or less kept as a private station for Crawshay Bailey, no one missed its closure, as this coincided with the latter leaving Aberaman House to reside at Abergavenny.

It was not until Monday 27th July, 1863 that the first permanent improvement in passenger services on the TVR took place when, for the first time on the main line, a fourth regular train on weekdays was added, together with a corresponding train on the Aberdare branch. Doubtless this was possible because of the completion of doubling the main line in February 1863. The timing of the fourth train, however, was of little use to the public, who needed an early morning train. Prior to the alteration the three trains had left Cardiff at 9.20 am, 3 and 6 pm, whilst the new times were 9.15 am, 12.30, 2.50 and 6.20 pm.

The local newspaper was full of letters complaining that the fourth train was of little use to anyone, and that people wanted a train leaving Cardiff between 7 and 8 am. It was little wonder that George Fisher reported to the TVR Directors on 11th November, 1863 that the fourth train was not remunerative, although the Board resolved 'upon its present continuance as a great accommodation to the public'.

In actual fact the fourth train was never taken off, and in its way was important as the first breakthrough in the painfully slow improvement of the passenger services on the TVR, and also that it killed the widely held view, in railway official circles at the time, that three passenger trains daily were ample for a 'valley' service. Sunday services were unaffected by the alteration, in fact it was not until 1896 that this service was improved.

The long suffering public had to wait a further 15 years before the service was further extended, although after that improvements came at more frequent intervals. On 2nd September, 1878 a fifth train was added, both on the main line and the Aberdare branch. At the same time the time for the journey from Cardiff to Merthyr was cut by 10 minutes. The main reason for these alterations was the introduction of the vacuum brake to the TVR, becoming the first of the local railways to adopt this system of automatic braking. Other changes of benefit to the public, at the same time, were the issue of return tickets at single

WORKMEN'S TRAINS

BETWEEN

Aberdare & Bwllfa Collieries

UP TRAINS.	Week Days.			Sun-days.	DOWN TRAINS.	Week Days.				
	A.M.	A.M.	P.M.	P.M.		A.M.	A.M	P.M.	P.M.	
Mill St. Platform dep.	..	6 14	10*37	10 37	Nantmelyn Platf'm dep	6 45	7 0	2 25	2 50	...
Aberdare Station ,,	6 4	6 23	10*46	10 46	Gadlys Rd. Bridge arr. Platform	6 58	7 13	2 34	2 59	...
Gadlys Rd. Bridge Platform ,,	6 8	..	10*50	10 50	Aberdare Station ,,	7 2	7 17	2 38	3 3	...
Nantmelyn P'tf'm arr	6 20	6 35	11* 2	11 2	Mill St. Platform ,,	..	7 23	2 44	3 9	...

*Does not run on Saturdays.

These Trains do not run on Bank Holidays.

WEEKLY TICKETS ONLY ISSUED
FARE 1/10.

Available between Mill Street, Aberdare Station, or Gadlys Road and Nantmelyn Platforms.

CONDITIONS.

The Tickets will only be available during the week for which they are issued. No luggage allowed except Workmen's Baskets of Tools or Food, which are conveyed at the Owner's sole risk. The tickets may be obtained on Saturday afternoons and Monday mornings at Aberdare Station, Gadlys Road Platform and Mill Street Platform, also at Aberdare Station on Sundays while the Station is open for traffic. Expired tickets must be surrendered at the end of the week or when re-booking. Workmen's Tickets are issued at a reduced fare, on condition that the Company's liability in case of accident to the holder is limited to £100, and the use of the tickets will be taken as evidence of an agreement to that effect. The right to refuse to issue a Workman's Ticket is reserved by the Company without assigning any reason therefor.

WARNING.—For opening a carriage door while in motion, or mounting or attempting to mount on the footboard or step of any carriage while in motion, or otherwise than at the side of a carriage adjoining the platform or place appointed for passengers to enter or leave the Railway Carriage. PENALTY—First offence £2 ; any subsequent offence £5. For wilfully or maliciously damaging any carriage or equipment thereof, or any property belonging to the Company, PENALTY £5. Any person convicted will also be liable to the Company for the amount of the damage done.

The Dare Valley branch workmens' train table for December 1921. Note that the two steam-cars are required to work the service, and that all afternoon and evening trains run empty one way. The Sunday night passengers would return by a Monday morning train.

fare plus two-thirds, and alteration to train times to give connections with GWR trains to and from Paddington at Cardiff GWR station.

A sixth train was added in February 1883, and a seventh in May 1888, whilst from 1st October, 1895 not only was an eighth train added on Mondays, Thursdays and Saturdays, but it was also announced that six of the Aberdare branch trains would include through carriages to/from Cardiff. These were put on the front end of the down trains from Merthyr at Aberdare Junction.

Return fares had slightly increased again by 1895, and as a comparison with when the Aberdare line opened almost 50 years earlier, the table below lists the single and return fares from Cardiff to Aberdare at the two dates. It must be remembered that return tickets were not issued in 1846, a single ticket had to be taken in each direction.

	Fares Cardiff to Aberdare			
	Single		*Return*	
	8/1846	10/1895	8/1846*	10/1895
First Class	4s. 0d.	4s. 0d.	8s. 0d.	7s. 1d.
Second Class	3s. 0d.	3s. 0d.	6s. 0d.	5s. 5d.
Third Class	2s. 0d.	1s. 11½d.	4s. 0d.	3s. 3d.

* Cost of single ticket in each direction

In July 1896 the service was again increased, to nine trains on weekdays (one Mondays, Thursdays and Saturdays only), and at last the Sunday service was increased, in fact doubled, from two to four trains each way. On 1st December of the same year the junction station for the branch was again renamed, being altered from Aberdare Junction to its present name, Abercynon.

A tenth passenger train was put on the branch in July 1902, and this was increased to 12 each way plus one extra each way late on Saturday evenings as from May 1903. This remained the basic service until steam railcars augmented the branch service as from 26th December, 1904. A remarkable change of outlook in regard to passenger traffic had taken place at Taff Vale Headquarters in the last 20 years of the old century, and when the steam cars started running the existing service was already vastly better than the older residents ever expected to see.

The revised service from the end of 1904 was 12 trains in each direction, plus a further train on Wednesdays and Saturdays only, and in addition 8 steam cars in each direction. The train stopped only at the main stations and terminated at Aberdare, whilst the cars, which mostly ran through to Pontypridd, stopped at the new motor Platforms as well as the stations, and terminated at the re-opened Mill Street Platform. In addition a few extra local steam cars were run between Mill Street and Aberdare station.

With both trains and steam railcars running, later changes were frequent and only examples can be given. On 1st October, 1907 the service was cut to 9 trains plus 9 cars in each direction, altered the following July to 11 trains and 8 cars. At the outbreak of World War I in 1914 there were 11 trains, plus 2 workmen's trains and 4 cars. During the war, particularly the later stages, the train service was cut

An evening auto-train for Aberdare Low Level leaving Abercynon in June 1957 in charge of
pannier tank No. 6417, from Aberdare depot. *J. Hodge*

An auto-train from Aberdare entering Abercynon station in August 1957.
S. Rickard/ C. Chapman Collection

back, and the steam cars were gradually replaced by auto-trains, these consisting of one or two sets, each consisting of two cars, according to the traffic.

No immediate return to the splendid pre-war service took place for many years afterwards, and when the GWR took control in the summer of 1922 the branch consisted of six ordinary trains, one workman's train and five auto trains. Throughout the period from July 1896 until GWR days the Sunday service remained at four trains each way.

One of the first things the GWR did was to get rid of the second class travel, which was abolished on the TVR, and other local lines, as from 1st July, 1923. The best of the second class carriages were upgraded to firsts, the others downgraded to thirds.

By July 1927 the GWR had increased the weekday service to 15 trains, or auto-trains, in each direction, with a couple of extra trains on Thursdays and Saturdays only. This had increased to 16 by 1931, and in addition a fifth Sunday train had been put on. By July 1934 the Sunday service had increased to seven each way, although three of these were run during the summer period only. By the outbreak of World War II the service was almost back to its peak with a maximum of 20 trains on Saturdays and a minimum of 17 on Tuesdays, Wednesdays and Fridays.

The war brought an immediate cut, and the service, as from the War Emergency timetable dated 25th September, 1939, was 13 trains on weekdays, (14 on Saturdays) and 4 on Sundays. This remained fairly standard throughout the war period, although an extra train was put on Saturdays only in the summer of 1942.

The summer timetable for 1946, dated 6th May, showed a recovery approaching pre-war weekday level, with 17 up trains and 16 down trains on Mondays to Fridays, the corresponding totals for Saturdays being 19 and 18 respectively. The Sunday service was improved to five trains, one of these being run during the summer months only. This service remained fairly steady until the Summer of 1952, when 19 trains daily was the regular pattern, with the Sunday service increased to 9 up trains and 8 down trains, plus a regular excursion through to Barry Island and back on summer Sundays only.

By this time road competition was beginning to take its toll, and British Railways made one last great effort to re-capture the dwindling passengers. As from 21st September, 1953 the existing 'valley' passenger timetables were largely scrapped, and a new regular interval service inaugurated. This, as far as the Aberdare branch was concerned, was mainly worked by auto-trains plying between Aberdare and Abercynon, with a few extended to Pontypridd. Twenty-one such trains were run in each direction, with five additional up ordinary passenger trains, two ex-Cardiff Queen Street, two ex-Cardiff Bute Road and one ex-Barry. In the down direction only two ordinary passenger trains were run in addition to the auto-trains, one to Cardiff Bute Road and one to Barry Island. On Sundays the service was nine auto-trains in each direction, plus two ordinary passenger trains to/from Barry Island during the summer months.

Unfortunately the traffic continued to dwindle, and by 1959 the service had been reduced to 22 up trains (1 extra on Saturdays) and 20 down trains (also 1

An up-valley dmu stops at Oxford Street station, Mountain Ash, c. 1961.

No. 5699 of a class of 0-6-2T built by the GWR and used extensively on the Aberdare line after
the withdrawal of the TVR-built 0-6-2Ts.   *Brian Webb Collection*

Another view of the ubiquitous '56XX' class 0-6-2T. No. 6665 is seen shunting at Aberdare Low
Level.   *H.B. Priestley*

A Penarth-Aberdare train in June 1989 passing Abercynon South station before stopping at the North platform.   *David Gould*

Set No. C984 at the re-opened Aberdare station, forming the 1.55 pm for Cardiff and Penarth, 27th June, 1989.   *David Gould*

extra on Saturdays), whilst the Sunday service had been cut back to 7 each way, plus the 2 Barry Island summer-only specials. The basic auto-worked regular interval service was more or less retained at this stage, although with the trains showing less and less financial returns the writing was on the wall.

The Sunday service was the first to be withdrawn, disappearing with the timetable commencing 10th September, 1962. To the end the service of seven auto-trains each way, plus the summer Barry Island specials, were retained. By the same timetable a drastic cut in the weekday services was brought in, with only 12 up and 9 down trains on Mondays to Fridays, increased to 18 and 16 respectively on Saturdays.

By that time, however, the service was under close scrutiny, and closure proposals were first issued during 1963. With the usual delays hearing objections it was not until early 1964 that the ministry of transport gave authority for complete closure, and this became effective as from Monday 16th March, 1964, the last trains actually running the previous Saturday, 14th March.

Thus passengers services ceased on the former Taff Vale branch to Aberdare after running continuously for 117½ years. The railway had been able to withstand the competition from the earlier road alternatives, first the horse bus and then the street tramcar. It stood its own against the early road motor bus competition, but the rapid developments in this field after World War II caused its eventual downfall. On looking back over the century of rail passenger traffic in the valley, it must be said that the Taff Vale provided a very meagre service when opposition was negligible. It rapidly improved the service at the first signs of effective competition, whilst the Great Western provided a very reasonable service during the years it had control. British Railways gave the best service of all, completely adequate, but not able to effectively compete with the modern bus services which had the advantage of passing through the housing development peculiar to the South wales Valleys, i.e. towns and villages adjoining in a continuous string, in this case an almost unbroken built up area from Abercynon to Aberdare.

Apart from Abercwmboi Halt, which closed as from 2nd April, 1956, all the stations and halts remained open until final closure. Abercwmboi was somewhat remote from the housing pattern, but useful in its day for workmen's services. For some years prior to closure only a few selected auto-trains stopped there. On the other hand, most of the auto-trains stopped at Pontcynon and Mathewstown Halts until the end, and of course all stopped at the main stations.

As mentioned earlier a passenger service to and from Aberdare, serving five intermediate stations on the branch, was reinstated on 3rd October, 1988. This provided seven arrivals at Aberdare from Cardiff, and eight return departures, on Mondays to Fridays, and a basically hourly service of eleven trains in each direction on Saturdays.

The increase in frequency on Mondays to Fridays to an hourly service from October 1989 has already been referred to. Some extra services on Saturdays between Mountain Ash and Cardiff were also introduced, for the winter timetable only, repeated the following winter, 1990/91, when the trains ran from and to Aberdare. A Sunday service was also introduced in October 1989, and has operated continuously since then, with the exception of the winter timetable for 1990/91.

In common with all valley lines services north of Cardiff, Sunday services during the winter timetable periods operate only in the afternoons and evenings, all-day trains being provided only in the summer service periods. During recent years the Sunday Aberdare trains have frequently operated via the 'City Line' between Radyr and Cardiff Central but currently (1995) this line is closed on Sundays, with the Aberdare trains reverting to the usual Llandaff route.

The current timetable provides departures from Aberdare on Mondays to Fridays at 7.02, 7.37, 8.03, 9.20 am and hourly to 4.20, 5.15, 5.37, 6.20, 7.20 and 8.20 pm. Departures on Saturdays are hourly from 7.20 am to 8.20 pm, and on Sundays at 2.23, 4.23, 6.23 and 8.38 pm. Other than on Sundays, most trains continue beyond Cardiff Central to Barry Island.

Arrivals at Aberdare are comparable.

During the peak hours on Mondays to Fridays when two trains operate in a given hour in each direction, the loop at Abercwmboi is used for passing trains. The normal arrangement is for up and down trains to pass one another on the double track section, south of Abercynon.

Valley Lines

Aberdare

Mid Glamorgan
COUNTY COUNCIL
PUBLIC TRANSPORT

Sprinter

Gwasanaeth trenau
3 Hydref 1988 i 13 Mai 1989

Train service
3 October 1988 to 13 May 1989

Chapter Nine

Locomotives and Engine Sheds

Engine Sheds

As recorded elsewhere the Aberdare Railway, at its opening in August 1846, had one engine only, the American built passenger engine *Columbia* and this was followed by the 0-6-0 mineral engine *Aberaman*.

The company erected two small timber engine sheds, one for each engine, on each side of the line immediately west of the town level crossing at Aberdare, presumably just of sufficient length to house either engine, which would have been locked up overnight. One of the sheds fell into disuse in 1847, because when the TVR took over the working of the Aberdare Railway the Aberaman was transferred to Cardiff Docks Shed. At that time, it was TVR practice to work all mineral trains from and to the terminus.

The other shed remained in use for the passenger engine, the first service of the day starting form the Aberdare end of the branch. Both sheds must have fallen into a bad state of repair as, on 2nd October, 1856, George Fisher reported to the TVR Board:

> I would call attention to the level crossing at Aberdare. At the time the line was formed two wooden engine houses were erected immediately adjoining the public crossing, involving the necessity of every engine passing over going in or out of the sheds. These timber sheds are now completely decayed and must be rebuilt. I would suggest removing the engine sheds to another part of the yard, more convenient for the company, and very materially reducing the number of times engines would have to pass over the level crossing, and entirely dispensing with the necessity of passing over the crossing on Sundays.

The last couple of lines of the report refers to the fact that the TVR did not work mineral trains on Sundays, thus if the shed was re-sited to the east of the crossing, nothing would have to pass over it on that day.

Nothing was done for several years, however, and it would seem that the branch passenger engine remained shedded at Aberdare, although there is a possibility that it was transferred to the shed at Aberdare Junction, opened in 1853; this would have meant running 'light engine' to Aberdare each morning to start the passenger service, and returning 'light engine' in the evenings. At this late stage it seems more probable that they managed as best as they could with the old Aberdare sheds.

Nothing further is heard until early 1865 when, following the vast increase in coal traffic from both Aberdare and Rhondda Valleys, Fisher reported on 16th March that,

> . . . at Aberdare a new engine stable is in course of erection, and at Treherbert land has been obtained for a like purpose, so as to keep portions of the company's engines at the various termini, instead of having all at Cardiff Terminus as at present.

In this respect Fisher was referring to the main line mineral engines, as his annual reports clearly indicated that passenger engines were shedded at Aberdare and Merthyr, and a pilot engine was at Aberdare Junction.

The new sheds at Aberdare were opened in the summer of 1865. Each was constructed of stone with slate roofing, approximately 100 ft long by 32 ft wide, the distance between them being about 140 yds. A coal stage was erected between the two sheds, the east shed being open at both ends, the west shed open at the east end only.

Each shed contained two roads and the sidings were arranged so that engines could pass from shed to shed direct, or for engines coming into the shed yard (from the east direction only) to by-pass the first shed and go direct to the coaling stage or the second shed. The west shed was tucked in the N.W. corner of the yard lying on the banks of both the River Cynon and River Dare at their meeting point. A 45 ft diameter turntable was provided near the S.W. corner of the west shed this also, of course, lying almost on the bank of the River Dare.

These sheds remained basically unaltered for the remainder of the Taff Vale Railway's independent existence, with normally some 12 to 18 engines shedded there according to the state of the coal trade. In the 19th century 0-6-0 mineral tender engines formed the main allocation, but from the 1890s onwards 0-6-2 tank engines gradually took over, although goods tenders remained allocated there until the end. At the turn of the century two of the powerful 'V' class 0-6-0 saddle tanks were sent to Aberdare, chiefly to deal with the traffic on the Dare Valley branch, and heavy mineral shunting in the area, and these remained there until after the GWR took control in 1922.

Following the amalgamation it was obvious that, with a modern well-equipped shed on the GWR line at Aberdare, it was only a question of time before the TVR shed would be closed, although this presented problems as the GWR shed was on the opposite side of its main line to the TVR line. At the time of the amalgamation the connection between the two railways was at the busy Gadlys Junction, and any light engine movements between the TVR line and the GWR shed would have involved passing over the junction, a double reversal across the GWR main line, and thence to the GW shed. This would have obviously been inconvenient with the still heavy flow of traffic in the 1920s.

It was not until late in 1927 that a line was laid direct from the former TVR line to the GW shed. This left Low Level line immediately west of the town level crossing, rising at a sharp gradient to the High Level main lines which were crossed without connection, and thence direct into the GW shed yard. It still meant double reversal to get into the shed itself, but this was in the shed yard and did not interfere with traffic on the main line.

These track alterations were completed early in December 1927, and the old TVR sheds were officially closed as from 5th December. By that time interesting engine changes, due to the amalgamation, had taken place, and of the 14 engines transferred to the GW shed, 10 were ex-Taff Vale, including the sole surviving mineral tender engine, two were ex-Rhymney Railway, and one each from the Barry and Alexandra Docks (Newport) Railways. Full details are given in the section on locomotives.

Both former TVR sheds remained in situ for a number of years, the east shed still being used as a stabling and watering point for engines between trains. The west shed was not used after 1927 and gradually became derelict, and in later years both were demolished.

Locomotives

The history of locomotives working on the Aberdare branch is almost the same as the history of Taff Vale Railway locomotives itself as, apart from a few of the smaller special duty engines, practically every TVR engine worked over the branch at one time or another. Unfortunately it is not possible to give shed allocations for Aberdare, as no such records appear to exist, although the early period is reasonably well documented, as are the five years the GWR ran the branch prior to closure of the TVR sheds.

The first locomotive on the branch, apart from any contractor's engine that may have been used during construction, the 4-2-0 named *Columbia*, was one of a class of engines built by Norris and Company, of Philadelphia, for the Birmingham and Gloucester Railway, and was purchased second-hand by the Aberdare Railway from the former in 1846. Two similar engines were purchased by the TVR about the same time.

Columbia arrived at Aberdare on 22nd June, 1846, and was the engine used for the ceremonial opening of the railway on 5th August. *Aberaman* was used on the Aberdare valley coal traffic for the next few years, but as traffic increased rapidly it was necessary for other TVR engines to work traffic from the valley as well. The *Aberaman*, with 16 in. diameter cylinders, was more powerful than corresponding engines built for the Taff, the latter being so impressed by its performance that it became the forerunner of a long string of similar inside-cylinder double-framed 0-6-0 mineral engines built for, or by, the TVR from 1851 to 1872.

Most TVR official reports for 1847 and 1848 which mentioned locomotives working the Aberdare coal traffic, revealed that *Aberaman* was at the head of most of the trains but, by 1848 at least, the 0-6-0s built by Messrs Stothert and Slaughter, at Bristol, in 1846 were assisting. This class consisted of four engines named *Severn*, *Avon*, *Clifton*, and *Bristol*; the last two were specifically mentioned in 1848-9, and there is little doubt all four worked on the branch at varying times. Three others that were mentioned in the 1848-1850 period were the *Cambrian*, *Llandaff* and *Newbridge*, built by Messrs Hick and Son of Bolton, also in 1846. These seven engines had 15 in. diameter cylinders only, but were capable of hauling about 100 of the wagons of the period, each of 2½ tons tare weight, and 5 tons capacity.

In August 1846 the *Severn* had hauled a train of 106 such wagons, total load 798 tons, down the TVR main line, and earlier the same day, 24th August, 1846, had taken a train of 120 empty wagons up the valley. The trains of the period were usually lengthy, and twice in 1849 the station master at Aberaman complained of the difficulty of shunting trains of such length on to the Cwmbach branch, and also of the trains stalling on the main line.

Reverting to passenger working, *Columbia* had little difficulty with the

The standard goods engine of early days; 'A' class 0-6-0 No. 273 (originally No. 78) built in the TVR workshops in 1869, in its final condition before withdrawal. *L&GRP*

'C' class 4-4-2T, built by Kitsons in 1888, showing the wire apparatus attached to chimney and cab, used when working auto-trains. *F. Moore*

branch passenger service which meant little more than 50 miles daily, and was usually replaced by one of the two TVR 'Yankee' engines, *Gloucester* or *Moorsom*, when under repair. By 1851, however, *Columbia* was in need of major overhaul and was transferred to light duties, then withdrawn and sold for £250, presumably as scrap, the following year.

The *Gloucester* was the relief engine to *Columbia* throughout 1850, and took over its workings completely in 1851, and an old 0-4-2 tender engine, *Plymouth*, built by Messrs R. & W. Hawthorn in 1841, acted as spare passenger engine for the branch.

Gloucester was transferred away from the Aberdare branch in 1852, and *Plymouth* seems to have struggled on alone until 1854, being replaced during repairs by any old engine capable of the work.

In 1854 one of the new 2-4-0 passenger tender engines, the *Dare*, took over the branch passenger working from *Plymouth*, the latter remaining as spare engine for the next 12 months or so, when it was replaced by *Dinas*, 0-4-2 of 1841 vintage. The *Dare* remained the principal Aberdare branch passenger engine until such records ceased in 1857. The 2-4-0s continued as branch passenger engines until the early 1880s, *Dare* was almost certainly the main performer until 1871 when it was withdrawn, with the *Cynon* taking over when *Dare* was out of action, but as the TVR had seven 2-4-0 passenger engines by 1859 any one could have been used.

Double-framed 0-6-0 mineral engines handled practically all the Aberdare coal traffic, until the later years of the last century. From 1874 onwards a modern fleet of 85 inside-framed 0-6-0's was built for the TVR, all but 12 at Messrs Kitson's works at Leeds, the others by the TVR themselves at its Cardiff works.

In the early 1880s, one of four 0-4-4T passenger engines, which had been crudely rebuilt from double-framed mineral engines, worked the branch passenger service for a while, but in 1884/5 three outside cylinder 4-4-0T passenger engines came out from the TVR works, whilst in 1888 three inside cylinder 4-4-2T passenger engines were built by Vulcan Foundry at Leeds, (three more later) and these engines all did a spell on the valley trains. Later the TVR was to rely almost exclusively on 0-6-2T types; the first of these, the 'M' class, comprised 41 engines built between December 1884 and March 1892. Their 17½ inch inside cylinders and 4 ft 6 in. diameter wheels made them ideally suited to mineral trains, but because of their large numbers, and the scarcity of passenger engines, they were often seen on passenger work in the valley. These engines were the pioneers of the numerous batches of 0-6-2 side tank engines used on nearly every railway in South Wales, the last examples of which, the GWR '56XX' class, did not disappear until 1965. Following the construction of 15 passenger 0-6-2 tank engines, in 1895/6, of the 'U' and 'U1' classes, these could also be seen occasionally on the branch passenger service. These engines had 5 ft 3 in. diameter coupled wheels, and where known as the 'high flyers', and generally dealt with the main line passenger services until 1914 onwards, when replaced by the well known 'A' class 0-6-2Ts.

After 1915 it was not unusual to see one of the 'U' or 'U1' class 0-6-2Ts

Three 4-4-0T engines were built in 1884/5 for local passenger services, No. 68 shown here was later renumbered 286 and finally GWR 1133.   *R.W. Kidner Collection*

The 'V' class was the passenger engine; this example, No. 23, was built by Vulcan Foundry in 1895.

working a branch passenger train, although none was actually shedded at Aberdare until after the amalgamation with the GWR in 1922. In the later World War I period the allocation at Aberdare was normally four or five of the '04' class 0-6-2Ts along with half a dozen of the older 0-6-2Ts, two 'V' class 0-6-0 saddle tanks, plus some five or six of the 'K' class mineral tender engines.

In the early years of the present century most of the coal traffic was still handled by tender engines, chiefly the more modern inside-framed 'K' class, although the last two of the old double-framed engines Nos. 251 and 252, were still working along the branch until withdrawal in June 1906. Although a few of the older 0-6-2Ts took a small share of the mineral workings, it was not until 1910 that allocation of new '04' class 0-6-2Ts saw the balance of motive power at Aberdare shed swing from the tender engines to the tank engines.

The '04' was an ungainly engine, with a large and particularly ugly cast iron chimney, and very large overall cab which seemed to dwarf the bunker. It was, nevertheless, a very powerful class of engine for mineral traffic, and soon ousted the tender engines, after its initial appearance in 1907. No less than 41 engines of the class were built between that date and 1910.

Mr Riches' steamcars, introduced in 1904, were unusual in having transverse boilers; they were fairly small (58 ft 8 in. including the engine portion), and seated 48. No. 1 was built in the TVR works, Nos. 2-7 by Avonside, and Nos. 8-13 by Kerr Stuart, this batch being third class only. Five larger cars, 70 ft long were added in 1906 from Manning Wardle. There was only one driven axle, but they did on occasion take a trailer, though this was against Riches' original desire, which was to avoid any running round at termini.

In November 1904 one of the small steam railcars was sent to Aberdare to open up the local railmotor service. When the branch service commenced towards the end of December 1904 two cars were required, one shedded at Aberdare and the other at Pontypridd (Coke Ovens). The cars seemed to be changed fairly frequently and most of the small cars worked on the branch in the first few years. Car No. 1 itself was reported as running through the level crossing gates at Aberdare on 19th January, 1907. Just before World War I the larger steam cars (Nos. 14 to 18) appeared on the branch, usually working with a six-wheeled third class carriage, with the front compartment converted to a driving compartment. About 1918/19 auto-trains made their first appearance, initially powered by one of the three outside cylinder 4-4-0Ts of 1884/5 vintage, and later by 4-4-2Ts but these were normally shedded at Coke Ovens.

Two of the six engines of the sturdy and efficient 'V' class 0-6-0 saddle tanks, Nos. 75 and 91, were at Aberdare by at least 1904, probably sent soon after being built by Messrs Kitson, at Leeds, in 1899. One was used on the Dare valley branch, both for coal traffic and the workmen's trains, the other for heavy shunting in the Aberdare area. Both were still at Aberdare when the GWR took control in 1922, but were sent elsewhere a year or two later.

The 'A' class 0-6-2Ts were of modern appearance, with short chimneys and domes and a large boiler with Belpaire firebox. The first engines of the class appeared in 1914 and no less than 58 were constructed by the end of 1921. it

Most TVR engines fell into various 0-6-2T classes; this 'O3' class No. 103, built by Vulcan Foundry in 1895, as GWR 430.

An auto-train in Aberdare Low Level station in 1956; the former south engine shed of the TVR can be seen far left.   *R.M. Casserley*

was in the latter year that engines of the class were first allocated to Aberdare, Nos. 408 and 412 going there new in January and February 1921. Thus when the GWR took control the tender engines were disappearing quickly, and the more modern of the TVR engines were firmly in control. The first known allocation at the TVR shed in GW days is given below, and represents the position as at 8th October, 1922 when a total of 19 engines were shedded at Aberdare (TV). The TVR engine numbers are given first with the allocated GWR number shown in brackets. All engines with TVR numbers in the 2XX and 3XX series were on the duplicate list, these numbers having been increased by 200 from the engine's original number, i.e. old 20 became 220 and 144 became 344.

Allocation at Aberdare TVR Shed - 8th October, 1922

				Class Totals
'A'	class	0-6-2T	140 (374), 408 (397), 412 (402)	3
'04'	class	0-6-2T	9 (282), 97 (298), 105 (236), 108 (310), 113 (317)	5
'03'	class	0-6-2T	155 (435)	1
'N'	class	0-6-2T	182 (494)	1
'M1'	class	0-6-2T	16 (503), 88 (483), 153 (567), 344 (582)	4
'V'	class	0-6-0ST	275 (788), 291 (791)	2
'K'	class	0-6-0	220 (923), 245 (928), 302 (933)	3
			Total	19

Most TVR engines received their GWR number plates in the latter half of 1923, although '04' class No. 282 and '03' class No. 435 had been renumbered at Aberdare in May of that year. All three 'K' class tender engines left Aberdare carrying their TVR numbers, numbers 245 and 302 to Swindon for scrap in April and March 1923 respectively, whilst No. 220 was transferred to Penarth Dock Shed at the close of 1922.

This was not the end of Taff tender engines at Aberdare as No. 357 was transferred there from Ferndale in March 1923, received its GWR number 984 there in October of the same year, and remained allocated to Aberdare Shed until December 1925. Two others, Nos. 917 (TVR 284) and 924 (235) were sent to the shed in November and December 1924 respectively, and worked from there until withdrawn in July and January 1927. The outstanding example, however, was No. 919 (298) which was transferred to Aberdare in December 1924, remained there until the old TVR sheds closed in December 1927, was transferred over to the GWR shed and, as the sole survivor of the class after 1927, survived to work from the GW shed until withdrawn in February 1930. One of the 'V' class saddle tanks, No. 275, was transferred from Aberdare to Cardiff Cathays in January 1923, but No. 291 managed to remain there - as GWR 791 - until February 1926.

Aberdare Shed lost its allocation of 'A' class passenger tank engines in 1924, these being replaced by some of the earlier 'U' and 'U1' class 'high flyers' which were still very useful machines, and wasted on the coal traffic to which some had been relegated after the 'A' class 0-6-2Ts had reached such sizeable proportions in 1920/21.

GWR engines were never allocated to the TVR shed, although many worked over the branch from 1923 onwards. The first to appear were pannier tanks of the '1813' and '2701' classes. One or two of the 'Dean Goods' class of 0-6-0 tender engines also made an appearance in the early post amalgamation period. A few of these engines were sent to the Cardiff Valleys Division to replace the withdrawn Taff Vale tender engines, but none were actually shedded at Aberdare (TV). They did not last long, the 0-6-2Ts being of ample capacity to handle the coal trains and, with their overall cabs, were better suited for the bunker first trips to Cardiff and Penarth, the tender engines leaving the crews far more exposed to the weather conditions.

The new '56XX' class first made their appearance on the branch in 1925, No. 5608 being sent to Abercynon straight from Swindon Works in February of that year. Most of the early engines of the class were sent new to Cathays or Barry, and worked empties into the valley, returning with the loaded coal trains, but again none were actually allocated to the old TV shed.

In the last year or two before closure some interesting engines from other absorbed lines did get to Aberdare (TV). One was No. 1322 an ex-Barry Railway 2-4-2 passenger tank, which had been rebuilt at Swindon, in May 1924, with a 'Metro' class boiler. Its duties at Aberdare are not known; presumably it worked passenger services on the branch. Two further 2-4-2 passenger tank engines arrived early in 1927, ex-Rhymney saddle tanks Nos. 1324 and 1325 which were allocated to the TV shed as from February and March 1927 respectively.

The last oddity to be shedded there was No. 1426, an 0-4-2T from the Alexandra (Newport and South Wales) Docks and Railway. At the time this engine was standard with numerous GW 0-4-2Ts and, as such, could almost be said to have been the only GWR engine ever to have been allocated to Aberdare (TV) shed. It was, however, an absorbed engine, and must be treated as such. In 1911 it had been sold by the GWR to the Alexandra Docks Company for working the Caerphilly to Pontypridd passenger service. In 1919 it had been fitted with a non-standard boiler, and in that condition returned to the GWR in 1922. It received a standard boiler again at Swindon in May 1927, and was transferred to Aberdare in October 1927. Being auto-fitted it worked auto-trains on the branch for a while, but after being transferred to the GW shed its duty was usually the auto working from Aberdare-Ystrad Mynach- Swansea East Dock-Aberdare.

The engine allocation at Aberdare (TV) shed changed considerably during 1927 as can be seen from the lists below for 1st January and at closure on 5th December. Three of the four 'high flyers' departed during the year, being partly replaced by the Rhymney saddle tanks already mentioned.

Allocation as at 1st January, 1927

Former Ry	Class	Type	Engine Nos.
Taff Vale	'04'	0-6-2T	279, 282, 317, 414
Taff Vale	'U'	0-6-2T	589, 590
Taff Vale	'U1'	0-6-2T	599, 600
Taff Vale	'M1'	0-6-2T	483
Taff Vale	'K'	0-6-0	917, 919, 924
Barry	'C'	2-4-2T	1322

Total   13

Allocation as at 5th December, 1927 (Closure Date)

Former Ry	Class	Type	Engine Nos.
Taff Vale	'04'	0-6-2T	236, 282, 314
Taff Vale	'03'	0-6-2T	410, 411, 417, 420, 435
Taff Vale	'U1'	0-6-2T	600
Taff Vale	'K'	0-6-0	919
Barry	'C'	2-4-2T	1322
Rhymney	'L'	2-4-2ST	1324, 1325
Alex. Docks	ex-GWR	0-4-2T	1426

Total   14

(These 14 engines were transferred to the GWR shed at High Level as from closure).

The next interesting stage was the closure of the TVR shed in December 1927 and the transfer of its engines to the GW shed, afterwards known simply as Aberdare Shed. The TVR shed had been under the supervision of the superintendent of the Cardiff Valleys Division of the GWR following the 1922 Amalgamation, whereas Aberdare GW shed was in the Newport Division. Whilst it remained a Newport Division shed afterwards, a number of its train workings, both passenger and freight were, of course, solely in the Cardiff Valleys Division. Apart from ex-TVR 0-6-2T No. 600, which was transferred away from Aberdare soon after the closure of the TVR shed, the other absorbed engines were all still at the High Level shed at the beginning of 1928, when the allocation was 57 engines. As this was an interesting period, and immediately before the new classes of 0-6-2T and 0-6-0PT appeared at the shed, the list is given in full:

Allocation at Aberdare Shed: 1st January, 1928

Type		Engine Nos.
2-8-0	(14)	2802/4/10/2/4/21/8/41/50/6/8/66/76
		3076 (ex-ROD)
2-6-0	(5)	2608/14/34/50/65
0-6-0	(2)	2399, 919 (ex-TVR)
2-8-0T	(6)	4258/73, 5236/8/41/71
0-6-2T	(8)	236/82, 314, 410/1/7/20/35 (all ex-TVR)
0-6-0T	(15)	769, 954, 1056, 1245, 1579/80, 1734/769/1829/56/68, 2113/59, 2742
2-4-0T	(2)	1414, 3584
0-4-2T	(2)	563, 1426 (ex-ADR)
2-4-2T	(3)	1322 (ex- Barry Rly), 1324/5 (ex-Rhymney Rly)

Total 57

A large proportion of these engines were not seen down the Aberdare branch of the former TVR, being used (especially the tender engines and large tanks) on coal trains on the former Vale of Neath line, proceeding to Newport, Pontypool and beyond. The 'Dean' 0-6-0 was kept to work the V of N Aman branch, approached via Gelli Tarw junction near Hirwain, at times when the water supply at Dare Junction failed.

Although the '56XX' class 0-6-2Ts, which had emerged from Swindon in large numbers from 1924 onwards, were principally designed for the coal traffic between the South wales coalfield and the docks, none were allocated to Aberdare until 1929, and the class never became numerous there. two members of the class had been to the shed fitting shop for light overhaul, No. 5650 in March 1927 and No. 5672 in September 1928. the first to be shedded there, however, was No. 5662 in October 1929. This engine was replaced by No. 6605 in June 1932, the latter being one of a trio of the class that spent most of their days working from Aberdare:

6605	(Built 9/27, Condemned 1/64)	At Aberdare	6/32	to	10/63
6628	(Built 2/28, Condemned 5/65)	At Aberdare	1/34	to	9/63
6652	(built 8/28, Condemned 12/63)	At Aberdare	8/32	to	11/62

One or two others of the class were at Aberdare for short periods, the three above seemed to be a permanent allocation. In later days, when the author remembers them, they were kept in beautiful condition, normally being on passenger duties between Aberdare and Cardiff/Barry, both by the former Taff Vale and Rhymney lines, the latter via Penallta Junction and Ystrad Mynach.

One further new class appeared at the shed during 1929, this being one of the modern 0-6-0 pannier tanks. the first to be shedded at Aberdare was No. 5729 which was sent there new on 15th February. further engines of the same class followed, and by 1935 these outnumbered the old 0-6-0Ts at the shed.

A couple of the small-wheeled 2-6-2Ts were drafted to the shed in the early 1930s, these replacing some of the older small four-coupled passenger tanks on light passenger work. The first to appear was No. 5520 in February 1931, remaining an Aberdare engine until December 1947. Another of the class, No. 4514, was there from October 1934 until July 1943. One further class to put in an appearance in the mid-1930s was the '72XX' class 2-8-2Ts, which were conversions of the '42XX' and '52XX" series of 2-8-0Ts made redundant by the depression in the coal trade. The extra-large bunker and tanks, which increased the coal capacity from four to six tons, and the water from 1,800 to 2,500 gallons, made the engines suitable for longer distance haulage than the 2-8-0Ts had been, although a large number of the older engines were retained, unaltered, for the shorter distance duties.

With new types of engine appearing, coupled with a drastic reduction in the number of long distance '28XX' class coal engines, the allocation at Aberdare shed began to take on a new appearance. In lieu of an allocation, a list of engines actually 'on shed' on 25th August, 1935 is given below, this being recorded by Mr P.J.T. Reed, a lifelong GWR enthusiast.

List of Engines at Aberdare Shed: 25th August, 1935

2-8-0	(7)	2809/10/3/31/62/80, 3036 (ex-ROD)
2-6-0	(1)	2667
2-8-2T	(1)	7205
2-8-0T	(8)	4214/60/5/85/94/7, 5229/71
0-6-2T	(10)	5609, 6605/52
		63, 65 (ex-Rhymney Rly)
		282/94, 311, 362/74 (ex-TVR)
0-6-0T	(15)	1245, 1505, 1530, 1769, 1846, 2739, 2793 (Old Classes)
		5714/29/47/86/96, 7751/73, 9712 (New Class)
2-6-2T	(2)	4514, 5520
0-4-2T	(1)	1420 (Old Class)

Total 45

The demands of World War II brought an increased need for coal, and the stud of 2-8-0 tender engines was quickly brought up to 15, which total remained fairly steady throughout the war. Two further classes of engine were brought during the early war period, these being the '64XX' class 0-6-0 pannier tank auto-engines, also one of the numerous outside cylinder standard 2-6-0s No. 5349. By 1941 only three of the older 0-6-0PTs were still at the shed, the modern version taking complete command of local shunting duties by that date. As the allocation remained fairly static throughout 1941 and 1942 the full list is given.

List of Engines at Aberdare Shed in 1941

2-8-0	(15)	2808/10/1/22/3/8/32/5/41/7/67/70/80/93
2-6-0	(2)	2677, 5349
2-8-2T	(2)	7205/42
2-8-0T	(9)	4214/28/85/97, 5237/45/58/9/63
2-6-2T	(2)	4514, 5520
0-6-2T	(12)	6605/28/52/93, 63/5 (ex-Rhymney Rly),
		282/4, 311/4/62/74 (ex-Taff Vale Rly)
0-6-0T	(19)	1585, 1716/69, 3610/55, 3747/53, 5747/70/87/96, 6410/3/37,
		7402/23, 7748/73, 9712

Total 61

Local mineral traffic remained heavy after the war, but due to the reduction of long distance mineral workings the fleet of 2-8-0 tender engines was greatly reduced. In view of colliery closures, however, the stud of eight-coupled mineral tank engines remained surprisingly high. By 1954 the 2-8-0 tender engines had decreased to eight, but the 2-8-2Ts had increased to three, and the 2-8-0Ts remained at nine. Even more surprisingly the allocation of 2-8-0 tender engines later actually increased again and as late as December 1962, with most of the local collieries already closed, no less than 12 of the class were still shedded at Aberdare, although most had gone by the end of 1963.

The early 1950s saw the gradual withdrawal of the 0-6-2 tank engines acquired from the amalgamated companies, and by early 1954 only two, both ex-TVR, remained at Aberdare. One of these, No. 282 easily held the record for the engine that was continuously shedded at Aberdare for the longest period. As TVR No. 9 it was certainly at the former Taff Vale shed when the 1922 amalgamation took place, and 'old timers' say it was shedded there ever since it was built, by Beyer, Peacock and Company at Manchester, in July 1908. As GWR no. 282 it was transferred to the GW shed when the Taff Vale shed was closed in December 1927, was rebuilt with a GW boiler at Caerphilly in July 1928, and then remained at Aberdare until withdrawn in June 1954. Standard 0-6-2Ts of the '56XX' and '66XX' series were transferred to Aberdare to replace the former Taff Vale and Rhymney Railway engines.

Following nationalisation of the railways on 1st January, 1948 the occasional BR Standard engine paid a visit to Aberdare in the late 1950s, but the author has no record that any were ever shedded there. A visit to the shed on Sunday 29th April, 1951 found 'Austerity' 2-10-0 No. 90630 'on shed', whilst Stanier '8F' 2-8-0s worked in on occasions. Amongst other 'strangers' seen at Aberdare in the mid-1950s was an occasional ex-LMS 2-6-4 tank engine, from Swansea Paxton Street shed; these were allocated to Neath shed for a while, and worked through on passenger trains. appearances by non GWR engines were, however, limited and to the end of steam the High level section remained essentially Great Western in character.

Mineral traffic declined rapidly in the late 1950s and early 1960s, and following the formation of the Cardiff Division of the Western region, Aberdare Shed was transferred from the Newport Division to the Cardiff Traffic District as from 1st January, 1961. After nationalisation the shed had been coded 86J in the Newport division, this was altered to 88J on transfer to Cardiff.

With so few collieries still open at the start of 1963, one would have expected the shed's allocation to have dropped well below the 45 engines there on 1st January of that year. This total still included no less than 19 heavy eight-coupled mineral engines.

Allocation Aberdare Shed: 1st January, 1963

2-8-0	(8)	3816/39/43/7/50/3/60/6
2-6-0	(1)	6361
2-8-2T	(4)	7209/14/34/47
2-8-0T	(7)	4252/7/79, 5237/40/9/63
0-6-2T	(13)	5624/33/47/9/80, 6605/22/8/51/61/4/73/90
0-6-0T	(12)	3603/27/55/99, 3753, 4688, 7423, 8723, 9600/7, 9731/47

Total 45

The long standing association of GWR standard 2-8-0s with the shed began to be broken in December 1962 when Nos. 2857/74/84 and 3822 were transferred away. Five more were sent elsewhere during 1963, Nos. 3816/47 to Neath, 3843/53 to Severn Tunnel Junction and 3850 to store at Swindon (later transferred to Banbury). A sixth, No. 3839, was condemned in December, but replaced by No. 2895, leaving but three at the start of 1964, Nos. 2895 and 3860/6. the first did not stay long, being transferred to Cardiff East Dock Shed in January, leaving Nos. 3860/6 to end the (almost) 58 year association when both where transferred to Neath in April 1964.

The number of 0-6-2Ts also dwindled during 1963; some were condemned and others transferred. Five such engines remained at Aberdare on 1st January, 1964, Nos. 5647, 6622/49/61/90. The '56XX' was withdrawn in March, and Nos. 6622/61/90 were transferred to Rhymney in May, leaving No. 6649 the last survivor at the shed. It was moved to Abercynon in September 1964. The solitary 2-6-0 tender engine remained at Aberdare until withdrawn in May 1964.

Shed changes of the eight-coupled tanks and the pannier tanks were frequent during 1963 and 1964, although the latter decreased in number during 1964 leaving only five examples at Aberdare at the start of 1965.

One other change worthy of mention was the transfer of six 2-6-2 tank engines to the shed late in 1963 and early 1964. The first to arrive were Nos. 4122/4 and 6158 in October 1963, followed by Nos. 4136 in November, 6144 in December and 4121 in April 1964. These engines took over most of the passenger working on the High Level line although their reign was short as closure took place as and from 15th June, 1964. Four of the 2-6-2Ts were immediately condemned, whilst 4121 was transferred to Severn Tunnel Junction. Engine 4124 had already been sent to Worcester in December 1963.

By the start of 1965, with the end already in sight, the allocation at Aberdare had been reduced to 15, 10 eight-coupled mineral tank engines and 5 six-coupled mineral tank engines and 5 six-coupled pannier tanks.

Allocation at Aberdare Shed: 11th January, 1965

2-8-2T	(3)	7205/22/53
2-8-0T	(7)	4258/68, 5200/23/26/52/56
0-6-0T	(5)	3610/99, 3753/96, 9615

Total 15

The shed finally closed as from 1st March, 1965 the final allocation being nine engines, the above list less Nos. 4268, 3699 and 3796 (transferred); and Nos. 3610, 3753 and 7222 (condemned). As pannier tank No. 9615 managed to stay till the bitter end; there had always been an 0-6-0T shedded at Aberdare from the opening of the first shed in 1864 until closure of the third, 101 years later.

None of the nine survivors was immediately withdrawn on closure, being dispersed as below;

To	Severn Tunnel Junction	4258, 5226
	Llanelly	5200, 5252
	Newport Ebbw Junction	5223, 5226, 7253
	Pontypool Road	7205
	Radyr	9615

With steam power in its final stages in South Wales the engines were not required at the new sheds and four were withdrawn within three weeks, probably without doing any further work. The others followed soon afterwards, the last being No. 9615 which was withdrawn from Radyr on 21st

July.

After the withdrawal of steam, mineral traffic in the Aberdare valley was worked by Cardiff Canton 1750 hp diesel electric locomotives, 'D68XX' class, with one or two 350 hp diesels for yard shunting at Aberdare. These were the first diesel locomotives to work into Aberdare itself, although as early as 1961 loading trials had taken place over most of the former Taff Vale line through the valley. The locomotive used for these trials was 'Hymek' No. D7012 which was on loan from Bristol Bath Road to Cardiff Canton at the time. The trials took place on the 11th and 12th December, 1961 when the 'Hymek' took loaded trains from Maerdy, in the Rhondda Fach Valley, to Abercwmboi. Further similar trials took place in the early autumn of 1962 when English Electric 1750 hp No. D6743, which was on loan to Canton from Sheffield, carried out trials in the Taff, Rhondda, Aberdare and Rhymney valleys. Diesel railcar sets of the suburban type had taken over the Cardiff (Queen Street) to Aberdare (Low Level) passenger workings by about 1960, but all passenger working over the former Taff Vale line ceased as from 15th March, 1964.

Following the miners' strike of 1984 the rate of pit closures increased and by 1985, following the closure of Penrhiwceiber colliery, Tower colliery, situated on the slopes of the great escarpment which marks the northern edge of the central plateau of the south Wales coalfield, was the only deep mine left in south Wales. Its coal was carried by an overland conveyor some 1,500 metres long to a loading point on the nearest part of the old Vale of Neath line situated where the former short branch into the adjacent Royal Ordnance factory began. Though the line had been singled, sufficient double track had been left on the Neath side of this facility to enable a class '37' locomotive to run round its train of hoppers before drawing them back through the loading point where they were filled one by one by a tractor shovel.

Then in 1987 the Penderyn quarry ceased sending out stone by means of its private line to Hirwaun station, and in the summer of 1990 the last recorded working out of the Phurnacite plant at Abercwmboi occurred. The Tower colliery coal was thereafter the only mineral traffic carried in the Cynon Valley.

The engine shed at Aberdare had been demolished in May 1969 and factories were afterwards built on the site. Some sidings were left in the station yard and usually one or two diesel engines were stabled there at night and at week-ends. The trackwork was reduced to a bare minimum, namely a running line with passing loop, and a siding for eventualities when the passenger service was re-introduced. Afterwards all the remaining station land apart from the trackbed and the old and new stations were sold for industrial development. The old station, having escaped demolition, was completely refurbished in 1994 for letting as offices, etc.

Although Tower colliery closed in April 1994, coal shipments continued until November with class '56's' standing in for class '37's' when it was necessary to take 36 hoppers instead of the usual 28, and the '37s' were seen double-headed from time to time. Coal production restarted at the begininning of 1995 following a management buy-out, and coal traffic started again soon after.

Appendix One

Summary of TVR (and Aberdare Railway) Passenger Stations and Platforms

Abercynon	First opened as Navigation House	9th October, 1840
	Renamed Aberdare Junction	May 1849
	Closed Temporarily 29th October, 1855-1st May, 1856	
	New station erected	1875
	Renamed Abercynon	1st December, 1896
Abercynon North/ Gogledd	Opened	3rd October, 1988
Pontcynon Platform	Opened as Pontcynon Bridge Platform	26th December, 1904
	Renamed Pontcynon Bridge Halt	2nd October, 1922
	Renamed Pontcynon Halt	8th June, 1953
	Closed	16th March, 1964
Mathewstown Platform	Opened	1st October, 1914
	Renamed Mathewstown Halt	2nd October, 1922
	Closed	16th March, 1964
Penrhiwceiber	Opened	1st June, 1883
	Renamed Penrhiwceiber (Low Level)	1st July, 1924
	Closed	16th March, 1964
	Down platform re-opened for mystery excursions etc. (later closed)	6th June, 1971
	Re-opened for regular service	3rd October, 1988
Mountain Ash	Opened	6th August, 1846
	Closed	January 1857
Mountain Ash	Opened	January 1857
	Renamed Mountain Ash (Oxford Street)	1st July 1924
	Closed	16th March, 1964
Mountain Ash/ Aberpennar (new site)	Opened	3rd October, 1988
Fernhill	Opened	3rd October, 1988
Abercwmboi Platform	Opened as Duffryn Crossing Platform	26th December, 1904
	Renamed Abercwmboi Platform	1st January, 1906
	Renamed Abercwmboi Halt	2nd October, 1922
	Closed	2nd April, 1956
Aberaman (original station near Aberaman Park)	Opened	May 1847
	Closed	12th July, 1856
Treaman	Opened	October 1848
	Closed	January 1857

Treaman	Opened as Treaman		January 1857
(Later Aberaman)	Renamed Aberaman (date authorised)		26th October, 1888
		Closed	16th March, 1964

| Cwmbach | | | |
| (V. of N. Section) | Re-opened | | 3rd October, 1988 |

Aberdare		Opened	6th August, 1846
	New station built (same site)		1914
	Renamed Aberdare (Low Level)		1st July, 1924
		Closed	16th March, 1964

| Aberdare/Aberdar | | | |
| (V. of N. Section) | Re-opened | | 3rd October, 1988 |

| Commercial Street Platform 1904 | | Opened | 26th November, |
| | | Closed | 1st June, 1912 |

| Mill Street Platform | | Opened | May 1847 |
| | | Closed | 21st November, 1852 |

| Mill Street Platform 1904 | | Opened | 26th November, |
| | | Closed (public services) | 1st June, 1912 |

The down valley platform at Pontcynon in 1962.   *M. Hale/ C. Chapman Collection*

Appendix Two

Growth of Mineral Traffic Originating on the Aberdare Branch TVR from Opening until 1871

	Tons		
1846	15,409		
1847	88,117		
1848	192,813		
1849	223,057		
1850	243,645		
1851	290,900	Coal only	246,539
1852	387,127		
1853	484,249		
1854	607,024		
1855	740,389		
1856	920,558	Coal only	850,416
1857	903,219		
1858	879,712		
1859	1,106,872		
1860	1,313,087		
1861	1,350,504	Coal only	1,311,986
1862	1,530,641		
1863	1,665,789		1,617,950
1864	1,472,075		1,432,202
1865	1,455,047		1,403,675
1866	1,630,937		1,577,654
1867	1,462,859		1,422,300
1868	1,498,306		1,472,053
1869	1,674,697		1,626,082
1870	1,585,319		1,533,406
1871	1,269,784		1,213,996

Dare Valley Junction in August 1959; the branch to Bwllfa Dare runs to the left, while ahead are Gadlys Junction sidings.   M. Hale/ C. Chapman Collection

Gadlys Junction, north-west of Aberdare in 1965; here in the early days the TVR had an exchange siding with the broad gauge Vale of Neath Railway.   M. Hale/ C. Chapman Collection

Appendix Three

The Dare Valley Branch

The Taff had, by 1856, revised their opinion on the prospects of traffic from the Dare Valley and in November that year submitted a Bill to Parliament to construct a branch railway from Aberdare to Bwllfa Dare Colliery, with a further branch from that railway, at Duffryn Dare, to Penrhiwllech Colliery (alternative spelling used). This Bill did not succeed, opposition coming from the Vale of Neath Railway which was already in the valley. Also from the Gadlys Iron Company, through whose land, adjacent to the Ironworks, the proposed railway would have to run. The Vale of Neath contended that as only three collieries were in production at the time, a second railway to serve them was not necessary. The combined opposition was successful in getting that part of the Bill deleted from the Taff Vale's Act of 1857. Two years later the colliery proprietors in the valley wanted to send a proportion of their coal for shipment at Cardiff, and requested the Taff to re-open the proposal to build a branch into the Dare Valley.

On 12th November, 1861 the Board were told that a new company, the Dare Valley Railway Company, had been incorporated to promote a railway line into the Dare Valley, connecting with the TVR (Aberdare Railway) near the road level crossing at Aberdare. This company was presenting a Bill to Parliament, and in view of the coal traffic expected from the valley, which would pass down the whole length of the TVR line from Aberdare to Cardiff, the Directors authorised a subscription of £10,000 to the new company. The Bill was introduced forthwith, and attempts were made to form agreement with the Vale of Neath and Gadlys Companies in an endeavour to prevent the expected opposition in Parliament. These attempts were not successful, and with time running out for the Bill's passage, the Dare Valley Railway Bill was withdrawn in Committee stage, the promoters announcing that it would be re-introduced in the next Session.

During 1862 a slightly different scheme, more acceptable to the Gadlys Company, was produced, and agreement reached with the Vale of Neath, the latter agreeing not to oppose the next Bill in return for concessions relating to traffic from the Aberdare Valley. This included a connection with the Taff Vale line, near Gadlys, once the Vale of Neath had introduced mixed gauge over their system. Thus the next Dare Valley Railway Bill, presented in November 1862 passed through Parliament with scarcely any opposition, and became law on 21st July, 1863.

The Act authorised a railway commencing by a junction with the Aberdare Railway in the Parish of Aberdare, and terminating near Bwllfa Dare Colliery, in the same Parish. One branch was authorised, from a point near Cwmdare Colliery (formerly Troedrhiw Llech Colliery) and terminating on Hirwain Common where other coal levels and collieries were being worked. The branch was not constructed, and was eventually abandoned by the Dare Valley Act of 20th June, 1870. The Dare Valley Railway itself would pass under the Vale of Neath's Dare viaduct, and the Act specified that if, at any time, the Vale of Neath decided to replace the viaduct by a solid embankment, they would have to provide a bridge, or arch, suitable for the Dare Valley line.

Although the construction of the railway did not commence until the early summer of 1864 it had already been agreed, at the half-yearly meeting of the TVR held on 25th August, 1863, that the Taff would work the Dare Valley line from its opening, paying the shareholders of the Dare Valley Company 5 per cent per annum on their investment.

On 22nd August the Board reported that work on the Dare Valley Railway had proceeded rapidly during the summer, and the line was expected to be opened at the end of the following month, although delays in obtaining traffic would exist as the colliery proprietors were still some way from completion of their connecting sidings to the railway. At the same meeting the shareholders gave their sanction to the provisional agreement, reached in 1863 between the Taff Vale and Dare Valley Boards relating to the working of the line by the TVR. The colliery sidings at Bwllfa were not completed until the end of June 1866, the proprietors apparently being in no great hurry once the Vale of Neath had laid mixed gauge on the Dare branch in November 1864.

The Dare Valley Railway officially opened on 1st July, 1866 and the agreement for the Taff working of the line became operative as from that date. It was not until four years later that a Parliamentary Act was passed authorising the leasing of the Dare Valley Railway to the TVR, this being covered by the Dare Valley Railway Act dated 20th June, 1870, a 999 year lease becoming operative as from 1st January, 1871.

When the line opened the Bwllfa Dare Colliery at the terminus was connected to it. The proprietors at Nantmelyn had not put in a connection, although a loop to that colliery was added in 1868, the two ends being known as Nantmelyn Colliery Lower and Upper Junctions. No direct link was put in with the Vale of Neath's Dare branch at Bwllfa, although connection between the two railways could be made, if required, by double reversal through colliery sidings. The only sidings from the Dare Valley line at its opening were:

a) three storage sidings near the commencement of the branch near Dare Valley Junction.
b) a run-round loop at Bwllfa, and
c) a short siding about midway along the branch known as Gadlys Ventilator siding.

Much of the branch above Gadlys was on an incline of 1 in 30, and worked under the 'One Engine in Steam' regulations. Very stringent rules were in force, up trains were limited to 10 mph, and down trains to 8 mph. A speed limit of 3 mph was imposed for any shunting movements at the collieries. All up trains had to be propelled, with the engine chimney first, and the load inclusive of mineral brake van was limited to 80 tons. Down trains, with the engine at the head tender first, were allowed up to 250 tons in favourable weather. The brake vans had to be fitted with life guards, sand boxes, and sand pipes at both ends. One strange rule, also given in the TVR Working Timetable for July 1873, was that the guard of every up train had to ride in the centre wagon of the train.

A workmen's service started on 1st June, 1904. Initially an agreement had been signed on 31st May between the Bwllfa and Merthyr Dare Steam Collieries Limited and the railway company to run a Contract service, the Taff to operate the service and provide the engines and rolling stock, the colliery company to pay a fixed sum monthly for the service. So heavy was the traffic that normally 10 or 11, five compartment workmen's coaches formed the train together with 2 old passenger brake vans. No platforms were erected but there were six recognised stopping places, two on the main line between the town road level crossing at Aberdare and Mill Street terminus, and four on the branch itself. These were:

Mill Street	- N.E. side of line
Town Crossing	- Through wicket gate W. side of line.
Glan Road	- Steps at N.E. corner of bridge.
Cwm Bridge	- W. side of line N. of the crossing.
Nantmelyn Crossing	- Opposite up home signal. Alight W. side of line.
Bwllfa Dare	- Beyond signal box.

The train started from Mill Street and was hauled in the normal manner to the Town Crossing. Here it reversed and the engine propelled the train on to the branch at Dare

Valley Junction, continuing propelling to Bwllfa. On the homeward journey it worked bunker first, at the head of the train, from Bwllfa to the Town Crossing where, after reversal, it propelled the train to Mill Street.

A fairly serious accident happened to the train about 5.45 pm on Friday 30th December, 1904. It was the normal practice to leave nine of the vehicles, including a brake van, on a loop between Nantmelyn and Bwllfa called Reservoir siding, the siding not being long enough to accommodate the whole train. The other van, with the rest of the carriages, would be stabled on a siding near Dare Valley Junction until near the time for the return working. The brake in the van at the Reservoir Siding was left securely screwed down, and the nine vehicles further secured by wooden scotches, in view of the 1 in 30 gradient.

On that particular day the engine propelled three carriages, with the second brake van at the rear, up the branch from the siding at Dare Valley Junction. On reaching the top end of Reservoir Siding the brake van was backed on to the train and the engine and three coaches proceeded to run-round to the lower (or front) end of the train. Workmen were piling into the train whilst this was going on, and just as the leading of the three carriages being propelled towards the front of the train was some 20 yards from it, the train started to run down the incline towards them. It appears that someone had removed the wheel scotches, thus with the two sections of the train moving towards each other the collision occurred, the end coaches in each section being telescoped and severely damaged, several others being badly damaged.

Many of the men on the train jumped from the coaches directly they realised the train was running away, and of the estimated 200 estimated to have jumped, about 40 were seriously injured and many others to a lesser extent. A claim for compensation for injuries sustained by a number of miners who jumped from the train was sent to the TVR by a Pontypridd solicitor in February 1905.

In 1914 the railway decided to alter the service from a Contract to a Statutory service, starting from the former Mill Street motor platform - closed for public services on 1st June, 1912 - cutting out the town level crossing stop, but continuing over the crossing into Aberdare station. After reversal the train ran back over the crossing and on to the branch at Dare Valley Junction. A revised method of working was introduced, the engine propelling the train from Mill Street Platform to Aberdare station and then, after reversal, hauling the train up to Nantmelyn. The return trip was similarly worked, the engine running round the train at Nantmelyn and returning, bunker first, at the head of the train to Aberdare station from where, following reversal, it propelled the train to Mill Street Platform.

A platform was erected at Gadlys Road bridge near the foot of the steep incline, and close to the former Glan Road stopping place, with a further platform at Nantmelyn. All the lineside stops were omitted, the train only calling at the three Platforms - Mill Street, Gadlys Road Bridge and Nantmelyn - and Aberdare station. This revised service commenced on 12th July, 1914, one ticket only being available, a weekly ticket priced 10d. permitting travel between any of the Platforms or Aberdare station. These tickets were only on sale on Saturday afternoons and Monday mornings at Aberdare station, Mill Street and Gadlys Road Bridge Platforms, also on Sundays at Aberdare station only.

At this point it would be convenient to record the official mileages on the Dare Valley branch.

Official Mileages - Dare Valley Branch

	Jn	Mileages From Cardiff Docks		Mileages From Aberdare Station	
		M	C	M	C
Dare Valley Junction		23	73	0	18
Gadlys Colliery Jn	DF	23	76	0	21
Gadlys Road Bridge Platform	-	24	14	0	39
Gadlys Ventilator Siding	DF	24	77	1	22
Duffryn Dare Colliery Jn	DF	25	3	1	28
Cwmdare Colliery Lower Jn	UF	25	12	1	37
Cwmdare Colliery Upper Jn	UT	25	35	1	60
Nantmelyn Colliery Lower Jn	UF	25	54	1	79
Windber Colliery Jn	DF	25	75	2	20
Nantmelyn Platform	-	25	79	2	24
Nantmelyn Colliery Upper Jn	UT	26	9	2	34
Bwllfa Dare Colliery Jn	UF	26	9	2	34
End of Branch	-	26	20	2	45

Only minor alterations to the timetable took place over the next 10 years, the train times varying slightly to suit colliery hours of working. By the summer of 1924, however, the number of colliers travelling had fallen, and it was possible to reduce the number of early afternoon return trips from Nantmelyn from three to two, the other trains keeping to the 1914 pattern.

The full service in 1924 was three up trains on Mondays to Fridays, two on Saturdays and one on Sundays, with dour down trains Mondays to Saturdays. Most of these started and terminated at mill Street, but at the end of the year Mill Street Platform was closed and afterwards the lower terminus was Aberdare station, by that time renamed Aberdare (Low Level). This did away with the reversal of each train (in both directions) necessary when the terminus was at Mill Street.

By the early 1930s the number of miners travelling on the trains had considerably reduced; the depression and consequent reduction of staff was mainly responsible although alternative means of transport contributed. In the summer of 1935 the three up trains still ran, although the number of coaches comprising the train had been progressively reduced to suit the demand. Of the original down trains only two remained, one to take home the night shift, 6.35 am ex-Nantmelyn, and one in the afternoons at 3.10 pm.

This remained the pattern until the end, although during World War II the late evening down empty coaching stock train was made into a service train terminating at Aberdare (Low Level) station. The full service in October 1947 follows:

Up Trains
6.30	am	Aberdare (Low Level)-Nantmelyn	(weekdays)
2.15	pm	Aberdare (Low Level)-Nantmelyn	(Sat. excepted)
10.00	pm	Aberdare (Low Level)-Nantmelyn	(Sat excepted)

Down Trains
7.00	am	Nantmelyn-Aberdare (Low Level)	(weekdays)
3.40	pm	Nantmelyn-Aberdare (Low Level)	(Sat. excepted)
10.30	pm	Nantmelyn-Aberdare (Low Level)	(Sat. excepted)

Apart from retiming the first up train at 6.20 am as from 1st June, 1948, no further alterations were made, and the last train ran down from Nantmelyn on 1st April, 1949.

The service was included, but marked *Suspended* in the Working Timetable from 23rd May to 25th September, 1949, but was entirely deleted from the next issue dated 26th September.

The workmen's trains were restricted to 15 mph on the branch in either direction, with further restrictions to 10 mph passing round the curve at Dare Valley Junction, also for 2 chains some ¾ mile down valley from Nantmelyn, and whilst crossing the road level crossing at Aberdare North. Sixteen minutes was the normal allowance for the 2¼ mile journey, this including the stop at Gadlys Road Platform.

The name Gadlys Road Bridge Platform was normally used in TVR public timetables, although Working Timetables gave it merely as Gadlys Road Platform. The GWR always called it by the shortened name.

After 1949 the Dare Valley branch was used only occasionally, the last coal being cleared and sent down to Dare Valley Junction in February 1957. Thus the track was in a state of disuse when the Stephenson Locomotive Society arranged a South wales rail tour, which included a trip over the branch, on 11th July, 1959. A three car diesel suburban set was used for the tour, and the day chosen turned out to be a typically wet Saturday in the valleys. All went well with the earlier part of the tour, and after passing on to the branch at Dare Valley Junction speed was stepped up on the 1 in 180 gradient passing the disused Gadlys Road Platform in readiness for the severe pull, 1 in 30 up to Nantmelyn. Unfortunately the disused track, and wet conditions, caused the set to stall immediately after passing the remains of the stone piers that formerly supported the old Dare viaduct.

A second effort was made, the set returning to the bottom of the bank and having another go. This again failed, the set stalling in almost the same position, much to the amusement of the numerous steam enthusiasts aboard, also a few local inhabitants who looked on the whole proceedings as good Saturday afternoon entertainment. Hence the Stephenson Locomotive Society did not get to Bwllfa, although it did get on the Dare Valley branch, and returned through Dare Valley Junction to explore a few more disused branches of less fearsome gradients.

On 22nd October, 1959 notification was received by BR from the National Coal Board that they no longer required rail facilities on the branch to be maintained. On the 4th December the same year the Cardiff District Engineer advised that the branch had become unsafe owing to flooding, following heavy rain, at 25 m. 58 ch. Accordingly he had issued instructions for the branch to be closed to traffic by clipping, spiking and padlocking the ground frame connection to the single line at Dare Valley Junction.

Once again there was no immediate lifting of the track, the negotiations took place over the next two or three years between BR and Aberdare UDC regarding the sale of sections at the lower end of the branch. Other correspondence took place between the NCB and BR regarding sidings and connections to Bwllfa No. 2 Colliery. It transpired that, under the terms of agreement between the Bwllfa Dare Company and the Taff Vale Railway, the former had met the cost of construction of both sidings and connections, but on completion these passed into the ownership and maintenance of the railway company, to be recovered and retained by them when the agreement was terminated by abandonment of the colliery concerned. The track was eventually lifted during 1962 and 1963. Authorisation was given on 8th February, 1962 and lifting of the upper section commenced on 7th May, 1962; lifting of the lower section started on 4th June, 1963.

Between September 1939 and July 1955 when reversal from the top end of the dare Valley branch to the remaining section of the Bwllfa Dare branch was possible, the Dare Valley section, from Dare Valley Junction to Nantmelyn signal box, was worked by electric train token, and the reverse section - the Bwllfa Dare branch - by wooden token staff. Nantmelyn signal box was taken out of use in December 1955 together with the electric train token and all signalling. A new two lever ground frame was put in near the Waterworks Siding (Nantmelyn) to cover the run-round loop and some catch points. The ground frame could be released by the Annett Key on the new Aberdare North-Nantmelyn train staff.

Following complete closure of the branch in December 1959, Dare Valley Junction signal box was taken out of use. This small box was still in typical Taff Vale style, with its elaborate end barge boarding, till the last. It was sited on the GWR side of the former Taff main line, in the short distance between the level crossing gates at Aberdare and the junction, from which it took its name.

Bibliography

Canals of South Wales and the Borders by Charles Hadfield
History of the Railway Locomotive Down to the Year 1831 by Dendy Marshall
The South Wales Coal Industry 1841-1875 by J.H. Morris and L.J. Williams
Pioneers of the Welsh Coal Trade by Elizabeth Phillips
The South Wales Coal Trade and its Allied Industries by Charles Wilkins (1888)
History of the Great Western Railway by E.T. MacDermot
The Great Western Railway Magazine 1908 and 1925
The Railway Magazine March/April 1947.
South Wales Coal Annuals (1908-1932)
The Cardiff and Merthyr Guardian (various issues 1844-1865)
The Cardiff Times (1863)
The Aberdare Times (various issues 1865-1902)
The Aberdare Leader (1902-1904)

Official Railway Books etc.
The Great Western Railway 1926 (summary of amalgamated railways)
Collieries on the Great Western Railway (1899, 1924, and 1932)
GWR and WR public and working timetables (various 1864-1971)
GWR Locomotive Allocation Books (various 1902-1963)
GWR Half Yearly Reports and Accounts (various 1864-1875)
TVR Board of Directors' Minutes (1844-1885)
TVR Engineers' Report to the Board (1846-1883)
TVR public and working timetables (various 1860-1921)
TVR Rules and regulations 1853
TVR Half Yearly Reports and Accounts (various 1876-1914)
GWR/TVR/BR(WR) various railway maps and plans

Official Government Publications etc.
Various Parliamentary Railway Acts
Ordnance Survey Maps of area
List of Mines (various issues 1888-1948)
List of Abandoned Mines (1919 and 1932)